D1029278

CRISIS AND DEVELOPMENT

CRISIS AND DEVELOPMENT

AN ECOLOGICAL CASE STUDY OF THE FOREST OF ARDEN 1570–1674

VICTOR SKIPP

Principal Lecturer in Environmental Studies,
Bordesley Department, Birmingham Polytechnic

CAMBRIDGE UNIVERSITY PRESS

Cambridge

London   New York   Melbourne

Published by the Syndics of the Cambridge University Press
The Pitt Building, Trumpington Street, Cambridge CB2 1RP
Bentley House, 200 Euston Road, London NW1 2DB
32 East 57th Street, New York, NY 10022, USA
296 Beaconsfield Parade, Middle Park, Melbourne 3206, Australia

First published 1978

Photoset and printed in Malta by Interprint (Malta) Ltd

Library of Congress Cataloguing in Publication Data
Skipp, Victor Henry Thomas.
Crisis and development.
Includes bibliographical references and index.
1. Warwickshire, Eng. — Population — History.
2. Warwickshire, Eng. — Economic conditions. 3. War-
wickshire, Eng. — Social conditions. 4. England —
Population — History — Case studies. I. Title.
HB3586.W37S57   301.32′9′4248   77–71426
ISBN 0 521 21660 5

To W. G. Hoskins
in gratitude for his writings

CONTENTS

FIGURES

TABLES

ACKNOWLEDGEMENTS

The research on which this book is based has been a co-operative enterprise. Since 1956, under the auspices of the University of Birmingham Department of Extramural Studies, and with the long-standing help and encouragement of Dr D. E. Gray, groups of enthusiastic and hardworking amateurs have been investigating the historical development of a compact block of five parishes situated on what was once the northern fringe of Warwickshire's Forest of Arden, but now forming the eastern periphery of the city of Birmingham. The research groups have had a gargantuan appetite for books and documents; so their progress has depended throughout on the kind and patient helpfulness of librarians and archivists. Special thanks must be offered to the staffs of the Library of the Department of Extramural Studies, of the Local History Department of the Birmingham Reference Library, and of the Warwick, Stafford and Worcester County Record Offices. Appreciation and gratitude are also due to the clergy of the five parishes for the readiness with which they have made the documents in their care available, and more particularly on this occasion to the Reverend Canon Harry Hartley and the Reverend Canon Raymond Wilkinson, successively Rectors of Solihull over the period in question.

From a personal standpoint I should like to record my thanks to the Governors of Bordesley College of Education, who, on the generous recommendation of the Principal, Mrs R. M. D. Roe, were good enough to grant me sabbatical leave during the autumn term of 1971, when the time felt right to begin hypothesizing.

Dr Joan Thirsk, Reader in Social and Economic History at the University of Oxford, has always taken a keen interest in the work of my own and other local history research groups. So it was to her that I sent the original draft of the text in the summer of 1975: to be rewarded not only by helpful comments and suggestions but with her own incomparable brand of eager appreciation and warm encouragement. I am also indebted to Thomas McKeown, Professor of Social Medicine at the University of Birmingham, for his prompt and detailed response to a particularly crucial enquiry.

ACKNOWLEDGEMENTS

When all this has been said, however, the paramount acknowledgement must obviously go to the members of the various extramural classes who actually carried out the research work; and especially to those whose names are recorded at appropriate points in the footnotes. No thank-you offering would be excessive for these sterling people: what follows is the best that I can do.

Yardley
October 1976

Victor Skipp

PART ONE
THE CONTEXT

1

THE NATIONAL BACKGROUND

From an ecological point of view, the most fundamental thing about the two hundred years of British history between 1500 and 1700 is that the population seems to have doubled in size; and the most fundamental question which an historian of the period can ask is how this major demographic expansion was accomplished. The issue is made all the more interesting, and perhaps all the more baffling, by the fact that our own rate of demographic growth during these centuries was greater than that of any other European country. According to the most recent estimates, the population of the British Isles went up from 4.4 million in 1500 to 9.3 million in 1700, an increase of over 110% (Fig. 1). Meanwhile that of Europe as a whole was increasing by as little as 42%, from an estimated 81.1 million to 115.3 million. The Benelux countries came closest to matching Britain's performance, with a rise of almost 80% (from 1.9 to 3.4 million). But the population of France edged up by only 22% over the period in question (from 16.4 to 20.0 million); that of Germany by 25% (from 12.0 to 15.0 million); of Spain and Portugal by under 8% (from 9.3 to 10.0 million).[1]

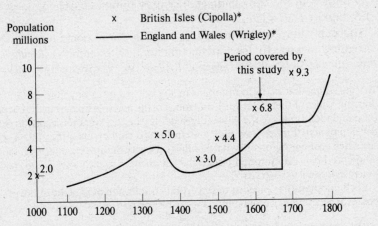

*For references see Chapter 1, ns. 1 and 2.

Fig. 1.   British Isles. Long-term population trends

3

Moreover, as well as outstripping her contemporaries, sixteenth- and seventeenth-century Britain was exceeding anything she herself had managed to do in the past. The population of England and Wales may have reached the 5 million mark about 1300, but was more likely in the region of 4 million (Fig. 1). Whatever the total, it proved greater than an overstretched medieval economy could support. By the early fourteenth century a Malthusian situation was developing. Numbers had advanced to the limits of natural resources as they could at that time be exploited: the land would feed no more people. As a result of the Great Famine of 1312–17, then of the Black Death, the population was cut back by at least a third, perhaps by as much as a half; and for the next five or six generations the prevailing demographic climate was one of stagnation. From the last quarter of the fifteenth century, however, numbers were again increasing. Until, somewhere between 1550 and 1650, the formerly crucial 4–5 million mark must again have approached, and with it the same Malthusian question. Would it be possible to break through the 4–5 million barrier on this the second attempt? Or would there for a second time be widespread dearth and starvation?

The answer of course was that a breakthrough was possible. By 1650 England and Wales seems to have had a population of at least 5 million.[2] Furthermore, this figure was successfully held for three generations; and then became the launching pad for the quite unprecedented demographic upsurge of the late eighteenth century and the industrial take-off which accompanied it. So much has long been known. What is not sufficiently understood as yet is how a country which failed to sustain a population of 4–5 million in the early fourteenth century proved capable of doing so three hundred years later.

The main purpose of this study is to try to throw some light on this intriguing lacuna. In his introduction to J. D. Chambers's *Population, Economy and Society in Pre-Industrial England*, W. A. Armstrong writes:

The questions that occur to historians in any age are apt to be influenced by the pressing issues of their own times, and much of the renewed interest in the historical population trends of the West is derived from the post-war preoccupation with developmental studies. How did Western Europe embark upon the path of self-sustained economic growth? What parallels exist with the modern underdeveloped world, and can the historian isolate the key changes in such a way as to enable practical lessons to be drawn?

Such questions have tended to be very much at the forefront of the minds of the post-war generation of economic and social historians.[3]

But how are such historians to improve our knowledge of the dynamics of development in the 'third world' of sixteenth- and seventeenth-century Britain? Unquestionably, one of the chief needs is for detailed case studies.

'The understanding of the demographic process . . . depends . . . on intensive studies at local community level', wrote D. E. C. Eversley in 1966;[4]
while more recently Richard G. Wilkinson has emphasized the close parallels which exist between small-scale investigations and 'overall national
economic development'.[5] With these considerations in mind, this book
has been conceived, less as a piece of local historical writing *per se*, than as
an essay in what might be called micro-history. The five parishes of north
Arden on which it is based may be regarded as a small piece of England in
a test-tube, as it were. Like the population of England as a whole, the population of north Arden was increasing sharply over the period 1570–1649.
Why did this demographic growth occur? What ecological problems did
it create and how were they solved? In particular, how *precisely* did these
rural parishes manage to support their extra numbers? What changes in
economic and social structure — and indeed, in domestic and cultural life —
were consequent upon the demographic growth?

'It is easier to demonstrate the existence of close links between population, economy and society in history', E. A. Wrigley warns, 'than to do justice to their analysis, for the relationships are very intricate.'[6] Nevertheless,
this book — drawing as it does on many years of research by large teams
of local historians[7] — is an attempt to do justice to such an analysis. Or in
other words, it is an attempt to work out a fully detailed model of demographic, economic and social change for one sample group of English pre-
industrial communities in a particularly interesting and crucial phase of
their — and of England's — development.

2

THE LOCAL SETTING

The contiguous parishes of Elmdon (1,127 acres), Sheldon (2,500 acres),
Bickenhill (3,771 acres), Yardley (7,590 acres), and Solihull (11,296 acres)
occupy a tract of relatively low undulating land which is crutched between
the River Cole and the River Blythe on the eastern flank of the Birmingham Plateau (Fig. 2). Formerly part of the Forest of Arden, this territory
lay on the northern fringe of pre-Conquest agrarian development.

The primary settlement pattern consisted of small hamlets, some origin-
ating as Saxon vills, others as colonies founded in the post-Domesday
period. By the time detailed documentation becomes available each ham-

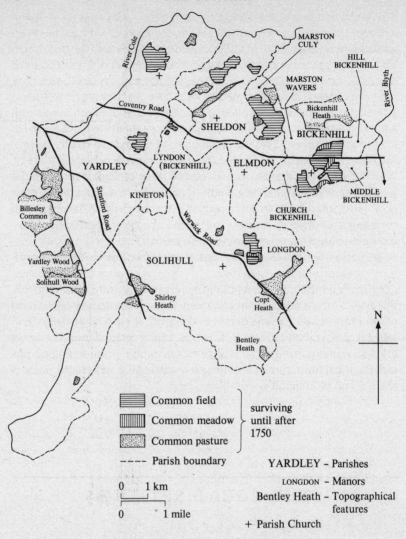

Fig. 2.   The five parishes — some of the main topographical features, c.1600

let is associated with an area of open- or common-field land, as is also the
planted borough of Solihull, which was laid out by the lord of the manor of
Ulverlei in the late twelfth century. The Warwick Road, however, marks
the limit of common-field agriculture in northern Arden. South of this, extensive areas of Yardley and Solihull were cleared by private enterprise
in the twelfth and thirteenth centuries, and so came to be characterized by
private assarts in severalty. This meant that these two large parishes had

a greater proportion of enclosed land than the others; and since severalt-ies were held on free tenure, they also had a much higher proportion of freeholders. At Solihull in 1632 there were no less than 75 freehold, as against 5 copyhold and 9 leasehold tenures.[1] At Sheldon and Bickenhill, by contrast, where common-field land had originally predominated, the majority of peasants held by copy.

Keuper marl, a heavy reddish clay, is the basic soil of the area, but over-lying this at many points are glacial deposits of sand, gravel and mixed drift. The founders of the hamlets, both in pre- and post-Conquest times, showed preference for the lighter soils, making their clearances either on small isolated drift patches, as at Mackadown (Sheldon) and Marston Culy; or on the edges of larger ones, as at Hill Bickenhill, Longdon and Greet. In general, therefore, common-field land utilized relatively shallow drift areas, while severalties were situated either on marl or else on the larger expanses of drift. The most barren glacial stretches, however, such as Yardley Wood, Solihull Wood and Bickenhill Heath, served exclusively as waste.

Many of the common-field hamlets developed independent manorial structures. The small parish of Bickenhill eventually comprised seven manors: Church Bickenhill, Middle Bickenhill, Hill Bickenhill, Marston Wavers, Marston Culy, Lyndon and Kineton. In other cases a series of hamlets was contained within the same manor and parish, as at Yardley, which, apart from the parent settlement, encompassed Lea, Tenchlee (later known as Acock's Green) and Greet. The hamlet of Longdon was unusual in that it had divided loyalties: although in the parish of Solihull, from about 1270 onwards it was attached to the neighbouring manor of Knowle.

As might be expected the peak of medieval demographic development occurred in the late thirteenth century, when the population density at Yardley was perhaps in the region of 1 household to 50 acres.[2] Though the fourteenth-century contraction seems to have been sharp enough, there are reasons for thinking that the depression of the later Middle Ages was less harmful and prolonged than it is reputed to have been elsewhere. According to a recent study, Warwickshire and Worcestershire increased their wealth between 1334 and 1515 at a faster rate than many other counties.[3] Lesser peasants may have found it difficult to cope. At Yardley in the early fifteenth century the rents of some of the smaller holdings had to be reduced, while others fell vacant for want of a tenant.[4] The more ro-bust or more fortunate members of the peasantry, however, were able to exploit these conditions to their advantage, systematically acquiring un-wanted acres until they had built up sizable estates.[5]

By the early sixteenth century local populations were gradually recover-ing. But if numbers were not so very far below those of the late thirteenth century, as a result of the tenurial and economic developments of the inter-

vening period, there was a marked difference in social structure. In the
early Middle Ages peasant wealth seems to have been fairly evenly distributed. At Yardley in 1275 only 3.7% of the taxpayers had been assessed
on movable goods worth more than twice the average amount, and these
leading peasants paid only 9% of the total tax. By 1525 8.6% of Yardley's
taxpayers had personal estates above the twice average mark, and they
contributed 25.6% of the parish quota.[6] At Solihull in the same year
Rycharde Greswolds paid £2 (on land), which represented 26% of the sum
levied; 10 out of the 129 remaining taxpayers found a further 25% between
them. Such families were by no means of great wealth, but they probably
exercised considerable social influence: the more so since seigneurial control, in the larger manors of Yardley and Solihull anyway, was inclined to
be relatively weak.

At one time several manors had been in royal hands or attached to a
great baronial estate, but from the reign of Elizabeth there was a tendency
for them to be acquired by nearby knightly families. The richest and most
prestigious of these were the Digbys, who, in addition to being lords of
Sheldon and Marston Culy, held the important neighbouring manor of
Coleshill, where they resided from time to time, and extensive estates in
Ireland. Hill, Middle and Church Bickenhill were purchased by the Fishers
of Great Packington in the mid sixteenth century; and Lyndon by the
Devereuxs of Castle Bromwich. Solihull was with the Throckmortons of
Coughton throughout the sixteenth century, but from about 1632 belonged
to the Archers of Tanworth; while Yardley, having been with the Dudleys
during late Tudor and early Stuart times, was acquired by Sir Richard
Grevis of Moseley about 1629. Although all these families had seats in the
north Arden area, the only resident squires were the Noels of Longdon,
and the Maines who had purchased the small manor of Elmdon in 1570
and the adjacent, but even smaller, Marston Wavers soon afterwards. The
not inconsiderable monastic estates in the five parishes all passed sooner
or later into the hands of local gentry. The Longdon possessions and site
of Henwood Priory went at the Dissolution of the Monasteries to the Hugfords of Solihull, and its interests in Hill and Middle Bickenhill to the
Fishers. The Greswolds of Solihull had obtained possession of the endowments of Studley Priory at Greet, Yardley, before 1600; and by 1634 they
shared with two other local families the lands in the same parish which
had formerly belonged to Maxstoke Priory.

Given the population densities of the late thirteenth century, it seems
safe to infer that, at that time, at least half the farm land would have been
devoted to corn growing. By the fifteenth century, however, with sparser
populations, the area had come to be characterized by a predominantly
pastoral economy, and this was still the case in the mid sixteenth century.

The average fully inventoried summer farm for the period 1530—69 is estimated to have covered about 33 acres, of which roughly a third (10 acres) was arable and two-thirds (23 acres) grass (Table V, p. 44). In other words, the mid Tudor peasant was growing corn almost exclusively for subsistence purposes; for profit he concentrated on animal husbandry. Due no doubt to the prevalence of damp clay lands, sheep were not greatly favoured. Instead, the main emphasis was placed on cattle: the rearing of calves, dairying to some extent, but above all at this time beef production.

Such an economy could support relatively few people. In 1525 it is estimated that the population density was still as low as 1 household (or taxpayer?) to 57 acres.[7]

3

THE ECOLOGICAL APPROACH

The main demographic, economic and social changes which took place in the five north Arden parishes during late Tudor and early Stuart times were described in a paper contributed to the H. P. R. Finberg *Festschrift* of 1970.[1] In the 1570s the combined population of the five communities was probably about 2,250 (Table X, p. 116). By 1650 there had been something like a 50% increase, to about 3,400. Meanwhile, on the economic front convertible husbandry had been introduced: so that it had become 'a usual course with the inhabitants to plow their ground which they doe call pasture for twoe or three yeares together, and then lett it lye for pasture fifteene or twenty yeares and then plowe it againe'.[2] An equally important economic development was the marked expansion of industrial activity. In the mid Tudor period such craftsmen as were to be found were invariably farmer or smallholder craftsmen who pursued their weaving, tanning, tile-making and smithery as a part-time by-employment. By the mid seventeenth century their successors had been joined, and indeed largely superseded, by a growing body of full-time landless craftsmen. With regard to social structure, the 1970 article demonstrated that, as a result of the price rise, the food-producing landed peasantry — small husbandmen as well as substantial yeomen — became increasingly prosperous; and here, as elsewhere, were able to indulge in the familiar spate of house improvement and refurnishing. But the effects of the price rise on the landless cottagers was the exact reverse, and by the 1660s

40% of local populations were adjudged too poor to pay the hearth tax.

The original study identified and described these changes adequately enough. What it did not do was to examine how they came about. In particular, it was not possible at that stage to establish the precise interrelationship between the various changes: or in other words, to analyse the dynamics of development.

The fact that this task can now be undertaken is due in the first place to the hundreds of hours which dedicated amateurs have given to research since that article was written; and which for three of the parishes has included the almost unbelievably punitive task of family reconstitution.

Of scarcely less importance, however, have been certain adjustments in approach and methodology. An investigation of this kind compels the enquirer to be local to time as well as to place: looking at developments not over centuries or half centuries but by generations. For it is only by handling the material in the strictest way possible from the chronological point of view that interconnections and causal relationships can eventually be teased out.

As far as demographic fluctuations are concerned, the key analyses, based on family reconstitution, were undertaken by quarter centuries: 1575—99, 1600—24, 1625—49, 1650—74. And the same 'generation' periods have been used wherever possible in the inventory analyses which provide so much of the basic economic and social data.

The ecological approach employed in this work developed gradually and unconsciously, having a lot to do, no doubt, with my involvement in the Environmental Studies Department at Bordesley College of Education. The moment of self-awareness came in the autumn of 1971, when the model was being conceived and I chanced to see a television documentary programme on ecological research in an Oxfordshire wood. One of the points this brought out was the way in which the owl population fluctuated in accordance with the food supply. In years when food was short some of the owls failed to breed. It occurred to me that this observation, to some extent, might also be applied to the people in the seventeenth-century Forest of Arden.

The main value of the ecological approach, as I see it, is that it fosters a sharper awareness than historians have usually shown in the past that man does not merely have to relate to man, but also to the physical environment. In ecological terminology, the early Tudor communities of north Arden, with their comparatively small populations and long-established pastoral economies, were living in a balanced relationship with their environment; while the unprecedented population growth of Elizabethan times represents a disturbance of this state of 'ecological equilibrium'.[3]

PART TWO

THE CASE STUDY

4

THE DEMOGRAPHIC CRISIS OF
1613—19

Detailed work on the demography of the five parishes has shown that, although there was an overall population increase of about 50% between the 1570s and the 1640s, the advance was by no means steady and uninterrupted. During the last quarter of the sixteenth century the rate of natural increase (i.e., the extent to which baptisms exceeded burials) was 45%. It fell during the first quarter of the seventeenth century to 21%, but rose in the second quarter to the exceptionally high figure of 62%.

The demographic rates derived from family reconstitution exhibit parallel tendencies (Table I and Fig. 3).[1] Closed family size averaged 3.5 children among parents marrying in the period 1575—99, completed family size 4.5. These figures dropped to 2.9 and 4.1 children respectively among those marrying between 1600 and 1624; then went up to 3.7 and 4.4 among those marrying in the period 1625—49. The average childbearing span, and also the average life expectation at marriage, follow a similar pattern, both being significantly shorter in the middle of the three periods.[2] From this it would appear that fertility was relatively high and mortality relatively low in the generations marrying in the periods 1575—99 and 1625—49, whereas in the 1600—24 generation the reverse applied.

A further variable that can affect population size, apart from fertility and mortality, is the balance of immigration and emigration: the effect this had on the number of childbearing families being of particular significance. The best available way of assessing population mobility from this point of view is by counting the number of 'reproducing surnames' (i.e., surnames occurring in the baptism registers) decade by decade. When the number of different names goes down significantly, it is probable that there was a tendency for more nubile people to be leaving the parishes than were entering them. When the number goes up significantly the prevailing tendency is more likely to have been in the other direction. Figure 4 shows that the number of reproducing surnames was increasing steadily during the last two decades of the sixteenth century and the first decade of the seventeenth century. At Bickenhill it goes up from 75 in the 1570s to 100 in the 1600s; at Yardley from 118 to 154; and at Solihull from 155 to 199.

THE CASE STUDY

TABLE I   *Demographic rates, 1575—1674 — Sheldon, Solihull and Yardley*
(figure in brackets gives size of sample)

	Couples marrying			
	1575—99	1600—24	1625—49	1650—74
A Nuptiality				
Mean age of males	29.7	29.0	29.5	29.2
at first marriage	(77)	(82)	(115)	(110)
Mean age of females	26.3	27.0	26.3	26.3
at first marriage	(93)	(98)	(126)	(123)
Percentage of brides	49.0%	39.5%	47.0%	34.0%
marrying under 25	(93)	(98)	(126)	(123)
Mean length of	23.3	20.6	22.1	21.0
marriage union	(94)	(127)	(132)	(112)
B Fertility				
Mother's mean age at	37.7	37.1	38.2	38.1
birth of last child	(18)	(27)	(32)	(32)
Mean childbearing	11.4	10.1	11.9	11.1
span				
Birth intervals 1—4	31.9	27.7	27.8	30.1
(in months)	(47)	(56)	(48)	(67)
Completed family	4.5	4.1	4.4	4.4
size	(53)	(68)	(60)	(64)
Closed family size	3.5	2.9	3.7	3.5
	(91)	(133)	(118)	(127)
Mortality				
Life expectation at	59.9	57.1	58.5	59.1
marriage (male and				
female)				
Infant mortality	133	148	147	130
(per 1,000 baptisms)	(592)	(460)	(460)	(338)

Mean childbearing span   This figure has been arrived at by subtracting 'Mean age of females at first marriage' from 'Mother's mean age at birth of last child'.

Birth intervals 1—4   For birth intervals to be included in this statistic the marriage must have been completed (see below); and either the wife must have been under 30 on marriage; or, if age at marriage is unknown, must have had 6 + children, which is taken as implying marriage under 30.

Completed family size   The number of children attributable to a married couple whose marriage was completed, i.e., the wife attained 45 in union or the union lasted 27 + years.

Closed family size   The number of children attributable to a married couple, irrespective of the length of the marriage union, provided this is 'closed' by the recorded burial of one of the partners.

Infant   A child whose burial occurs within one year of baptism; or, if no baptism is recorded, is described as an infant in the burial register.

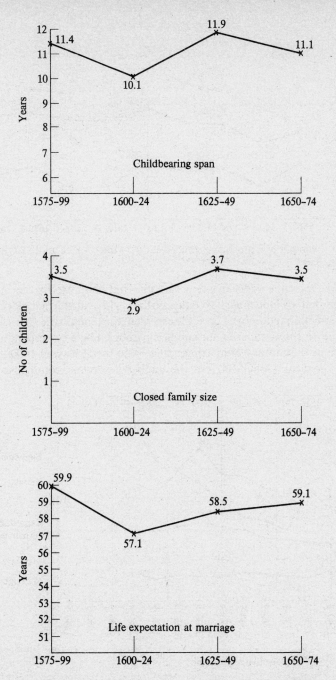

Fig. 3.   Selected demographic rates, 1575—1674 — Sheldon, Solihull and Yardley (see Table I)

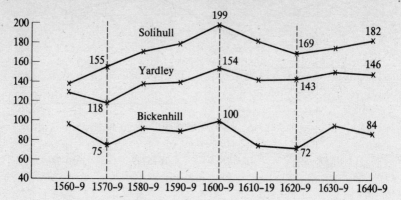

Fig. 4.   Number of reproducing surnames, 1560–1649 – Bickenhill, Solihull and Yardley

Often the appearance of a new surname in the baptism register simply means that a single male has come into the parish and married a local girl. This may frequently have been the case from the 1550s to the 1580s, when the rise in the number of surnames is paralleled by a corresponding increase in the number of marriages (Fig. 5). In the 1590s and 1600s, however, the picture looks different: the number of surnames continues to rise,

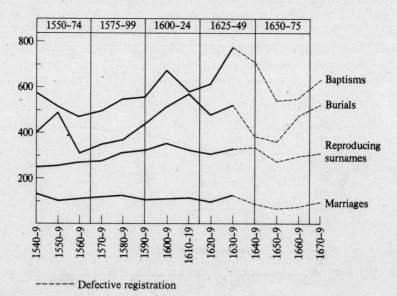

Fig. 5.   Decadal totals of baptisms, marriages, burials and reproducing surnames, 1540s to 1670s – Solihull and Yardley

but the number of marriages actually declines. Over this twenty-year period, therefore, it seems as if married couples – doubtless sometimes already with children – rather than single males were bringing the new names into the parishes.

Detailed work on the Solihull registers tends to confirm these deductions. Over the quarter century 1600–24, 127 fathers of families had three or more entries associated with them. Only 48 of this 127 were christened at Solihull; 79 were apparently newcomers. Furthermore, of the latter, only 21 were married at Solihull; 58, or over 70%, make their first appearance in connection with the baptism or burial of a child.

The place of origin of foreigners is rarely stated. It may be of significance, however, that all 8 located immigrants who make their first appearance in the Solihull registers between 1607 and 1615 are known to have come from the east, 3 of them directly from the comparatively remote borderlands of Northamptonshire, Oxfordshire and Buckinghamshire, an area which – unlike the Arden itself – was affected by the Midland Revolt of 1607 (Fig. 6).

Certainly it must have been the presence of so many new families which caused what almost looks like a baby boom in the first decade of the seven-

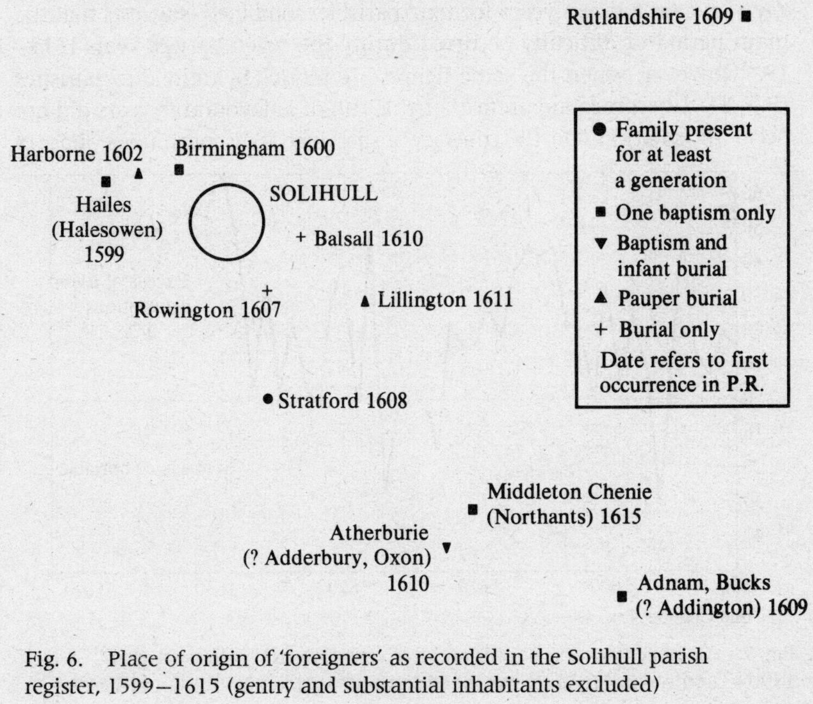

Fig. 6. Place of origin of 'foreigners' as recorded in the Solihull parish register, 1599–1615 (gentry and substantial inhabitants excluded)

teenth century, at a time when family reconstitution — as represented by
closed and completed family size, etc. — makes it look most unlikely that
abnormally high fertility could have been responsible. In the 1570s an
average of 65 baptisms are recorded for the five parishes per annum; the
corresponding figure for the 1600s is 92. The corrected Cox estimate of
population size, which is derived from these figures, works out at about
3,100 for the 1600s, as against 2,250 for the 1570s.[3] On this reckoning, the
combination of vigorous internal growth and steady immigration had
produced a 38% population increase in thirty years.

In the second decade of the seventeenth century, however, the demographic climate changes dramatically. By the 1620s the number of reproducing surnames has dropped a full 15% — from 453 to 384 (Fig. 4). Moreover, down to this time, from as far back as the 1560s, the decadal totals
of baptisms and burials had always moved more or less in accord with
each other, and in such a way as to leave a pronounced excess of baptisms
(Fig. 5). But in the 1610s baptisms fall to an average of 80 per annum;
while burials, which had averaged 65 per annum in the 1600s, rise to 73
per annum. This means that the natural increase rate for the 1610s was a
mere 9.4%, as against 40% in the previous decade.

Figure 7, which shows the excess of live conceptions over burials, or
vice versa, by harvest years for four parishes combined, suggests that the
main period of difficulty occurred during the seven harvest years 1613—
19.[4] However, when the same figures are plotted by individual parishes
(Fig. 8), it becomes apparent that this run of unfavourable years did not
occur in isolation. On the contrary, a sustained if discontinuous phase of

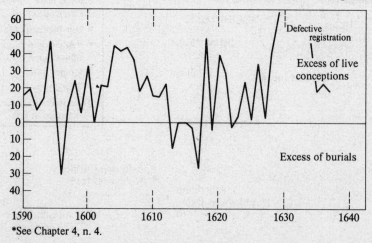

*See Chapter 4, n. 4.

Fig. 7.   Balance between burials and live conceptions* by harvest year*,
1590—1640 — combined figures for Bickenhill, Sheldon, Solihull and Yardley

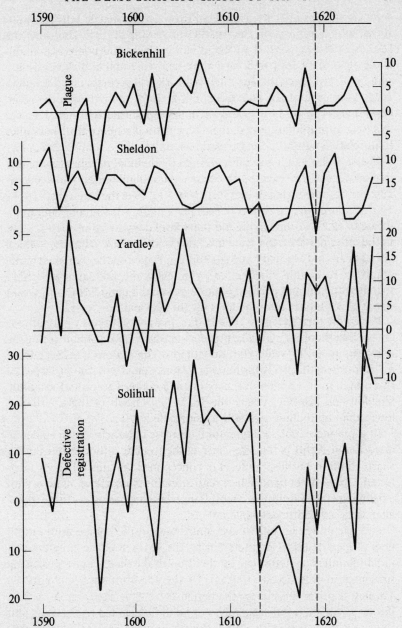

Fig. 8.   Balance between burials and live conceptions by harvest year, 1590–1625 — individual parishes (plottings below base lines indicate excess of burials, those above indicate excess of conceptions)

demographic instability was ushered in by the national dearth of the mid-1590s, which affected all the parishes to varying degrees. Thereafter the 1602 harvest year saw an excess of burials over conceptions at Solihull, while at Yardley 1601 and 1608 were bad years, and at Bickenhill 1601 and 1603. Two decades later such years are still occurring: at Solihull in 1623, Yardley in 1624 and Bickenhill in 1625. Nevertheless, the seven harvest years 1613—19 do stand out as being particularly critical. For over this long unpropitious period, there is no natural increase at all, but rather a cumulative natural decrease of almost 6%.

Figure 9 shows the mortality record of individual parishes for the first two decades of the seventeenth century. At Solihull burials had averaged 28.2 per annum during the ten years 1603—12. Over the seven years 1613—19 this figure goes up to 40.1 burials per annum, which represents an increase of 42.2%. Although the mortality level does not climb to this extent in the other parishes, the same tendency is in evidence. Thus the Solihull burial peaks of 1613, 1617 and 1619 are duplicated on the combined burial graph for Bickenhill, Sheldon and Yardley; while, taking these parishes together, the annual average of burials over the period 1613—19 works out at 13.9% higher than the level for the previous ten years.

If we now turn to Figure 10 recording live conceptions by harvest year we see that there is a particularly pronounced trough at Solihull during the five years 1613—17, when the annual rate of conceptions was 26.3% down on the mean of the preceding ten years. Moreover, as with the burial peaks, this trough in conceptions is echoed on the combined graph for Bickenhill, Sheldon and Yardley; where the 1613—17 shortfall of 16.8%, although lower than at Solihull, was still considerable.

In a pre-industrial society natural decrease often arises from epidemic disease. But if this is the sole cause of the trouble, although one finds a sharp climb in burials, the level of conceptions remains relatively unaffected. On the other hand, where high mortality is associated, as here, with a below average number of conceptions it becomes necessary to search for alternative or additional explanations.

One factor which must have contributed to the comparative emptiness of local baptism registers during the 1610s was the emigration of nubile families, as indicated by the drop in the number of reproducing surnames in this decade (Fig. 4). Of the 156 surnames found in the Yardley baptism register for the period 1600—9 as many as 31, or 20%, do not occur there subsequently. For Solihull, detailed registration, plus the availability of extensive supporting documentation, makes it possible to sort a considerable proportion of the inhabitants into one of three categories. Those who are specified as landholders in manorial surveys, have an inventoried estate worth more than a quarter of the average, pay pew

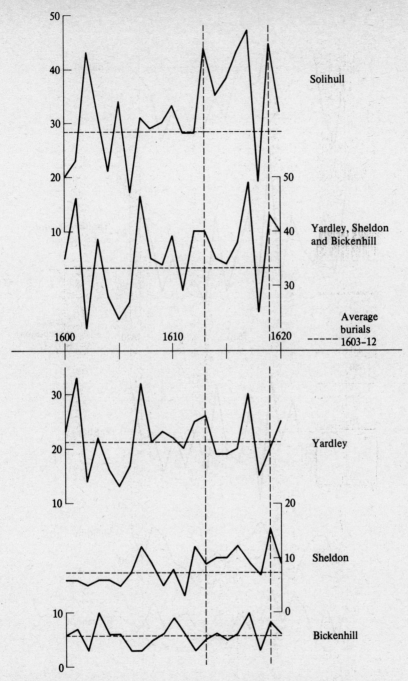

Fig. 9. Burials by harvest year, 1600—20 — Solihull, Yardley, Sheldon and Bickenhill

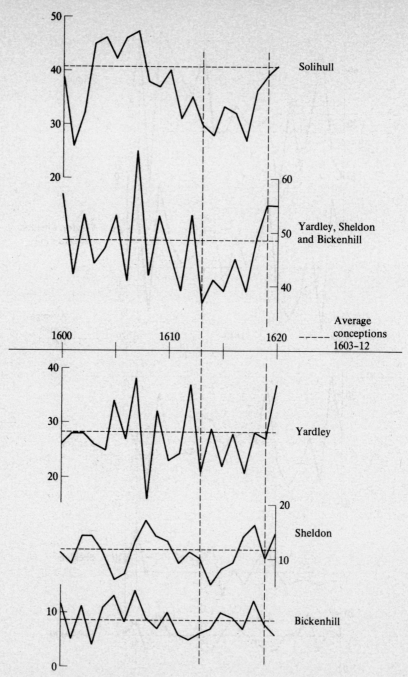

Fig. 10. Live conceptions by harvest year, 1600—20 — Solihull, Yardley, Sheldon and Bickenhill

rent, serve as parish officers or as appraisers of a fellow parishioner's inventory may be categorized as 'landed'. At the other end of the social and economic spectrum, inhabitants having tenements of under 1 acre, receiving Wheatly's dole for 'decayed tradesmen' (see p. 55), or being described in the burial register as paupers can be assumed for the most part to have been 'landless'; and to this group also may be allocated a handful of families with unusual names and strong cottager or pauper associations. The third group consists of people who, although they are not identifiable as paupers, recipients of Wheatly's dole or cottagers, are not to be found in manorial surveys either, or among those paying pew rent, serving as parish officers or appraisers.[5] Some of these 'doubtful' inhabitants may have held sizable sub-tenancies and been relatively prosperous; but the majority are likely to have been landless cottagers.

An analysis of the family reconstitution sheets for the 1600—24 marriage cohort shows that among identifiable landed families one or both marriage partners are buried at Solihull in 28 out of 30 cases. The identifiably landless were almost as static, for of 26 such couples all but 3 ended their marriage union within the parish. Indeed, in the case of paupers we should not have known of their status had they not done so. Among the 'doubtful', however, the situation is different: no less than 14 out of their 18 reconstitution sheets, although detailing a marriage and usually one or more baptisms, fail to record the burial of either partner. Many of these families probably left Solihull in the 1610s, and in so far as they did so during the procreative phase of their marriage, this would obviously tend to deplete the baptism register.

However, under normal circumstances, one would expect a fall in baptisms, if caused solely by emigration, to be counterbalanced — and in terms of natural increase, even cancelled out — by a proportionate decline in the number of burials; and with the high mortality record of the 1610s it would be difficult to argue that this was in fact the case.

Bearing in mind the low closed and completed family sizes among parents marrying between 1600 and 1624, a second possible factor in accounting for the low birth-rate during the 1613—17 period would be a temporary decline in fertility. Table II gives age-specific marital fertility rates for four successive generations, while Figure 11 represents them on a graph. It will be seen that women marrying in the first quarter of the seventeenth century were in fact substantially less fertile than their counterparts in other cohorts for every age group — with only one minor exception. The extremely poor showing of women aged 25—9 is particularly significant since, as a rule, and indeed for the other three generations, this is a time of peak fertility.

It is generally argued that when an age-specific marital fertility plotting

TABLE II *Age-specific marital fertility, 1575–1674 – Sheldon, Solihull and Yardley (children born per 1,000 woman-years lived – figure in brackets gives number of woman-years on which the rate is based*)*

Age-group of wife	Couples marrying			
	1575–99	1600–24	1625–49	1650–74
15–19	667	462	235	444
	(7.5)	(6.5)	(8.5)	(4.5)
20–4	417	393	432	358
	(57.5)	(58.5)	(95.0)	(47.5)
25–9	424	337	459	435
	(92.0)	(139.5)	(185.0)	(142.5)
30–4	312	339	377	366
	(112.0)	(159.0)	(204.0)	(218.5)
35–9	228	204	258	270
	(101.0)	(142.0)	(201.5)	(196.0)
40–4	175	112	150	186
	(74.5)	(132.5)	(172.5)	(150.5)
45–9	50	40	34	15
	(60.5)	(95.0)	(145.0)	(135.0)

*i.e. the total number of nuptial years lived by observed women during the age-range covered by each sample.

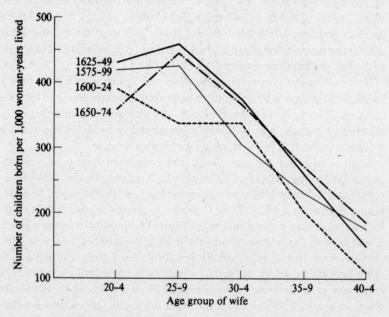

Fig. 11. Age-specific marital fertility, 1525–1674 – Sheldon, Solihull and Yardley (see Table II)

takes the form of a fully convex curve this implies that the rate of conception among the women concerned was more or less natural and uninhibited. The graphs for the fertile 1625—49 and 1650—74 generations conform to this pattern. The 1575—99 and 1600—24 curves, by contrast, exhibit unmistakable concave tendencies, a characteristic which has usually been assumed to indicate that some form of family limitation was being practised. If this were indeed the case, however, it would be a century and a half earlier than at Crulai in France, and half a century earlier than Dr Wrigley claims it to have been practised at Colyton.[6] In any case, when the various supplementary tests which Dr Wrigley used to confirm birth control are carried out for the 1600—24 Arden cohort, the results are almost entirely negative (see Appendix I).

Recent medical research, on the other hand, has introduced the possibility that a sagging age-specific marital fertility curve might equally well be caused by undernourishment: which can both inhibit ovulation and increase the incidence of miscarriages. Professor McKeown writes:

There are many different kinds of influences which may affect the likelihood of conception after intercourse. One class comprises the stresses imposed by the external environment, of which the most important is undoubtedly deficient food . . . there is reason to believe that the effects of insufficient food on fertility are profound. It has been shown recently that in young women in developed countries a minimum weight for height is necessary both for the menarche and for the maintenance of the menstrual cycle, and relatively modest weight losses result in amenorrhoea. This suggests that in developing countries today, among women not using contraceptives the number of pregnancies is probably limited more by lack of food than by practices such as prolonged lactation . . . It also seems likely that poor nutrition was an important cause of infertility in early populations.[7]

Against this background, the coincidence of wave-crests of burials in 1613 and 1617 with a five-year trough of conceptions, inevitably makes one wonder whether a dearth of food may not have been partly responsible for the Arden crisis of the 1610s. It would obviously be helpful in testing this hypothesis further if age-specific fertility rates could be established for landed and landless families separately, since it could then be seen whether, as one would anticipate, the ill effects were confined to the latter. Unfortunately, since families cannot be included unless the age of the mother is known, the samples available for this purpose are extremely small; and age-specific marital fertility figures based on much less than 100 woman-years can certainly not be regarded as dependable. Nevertheless Table III and Figure 12 provide the results of such an analysis, which in the circumstances turn out to be almost embarrassingly affirmatory. As will be seen, the curve representing 10 fully documented landed families which were formed 1600—24 is convex and exceptionally high

TABLE III   *Age-specific marital fertility in landed and landless families, 1600—49 — Sheldon, Solihull and Yardley (children born per 1,000 woman-years lived — figure in brackets gives number of woman-years on which the rate is based)*

Age-group of wife	Couples marrying			
	1600—24		1625—49	
	Landed (10 families)	Landless (9 families)	Landed (19 families)	Landless (11 families)
20—4	514	350	460	455
	(11.5)	(8.5)	(37.0)	(6.5)
25—9	493	256	435	418
	(38.5)	(19.5)	(69.0)	(28.5)
30—4	449	265	349	325
	(38.0)	(26.5)	(69.0)	(52.0)
35—9	286	182	230	225
	(35.0)	(22.5)	(74.0)	(40.0)
40—4	171	80	160	111
	(35.0)	(25.0)	(75.0)	(27.0)
45—9	57	0	27	0
	(35.0)	(18.5)	(73.5)	(15.0)

(the sample, as it happened, included families of 11, 10, 9 and 8 children). The curve derived from 9 landless marriages is concave and quite unusually low. Moreover, comparison of the last curve with that of landless families in the 1625—49 cohort suggests that this particularly emphatic contrast between the fertility rates of rich and poor may have been exceptional rather than a long-term demographic feature.

Other evidence which can be derived from family reconstitution has a slightly sounder statistical base. Table IV confirms that landed families started during the first quarter of the seventeenth century were unaffected by the difficulties of the 1610s, their average length of marriage union, childbearing span, birth intervals and closed family size being much the same as in other periods. Among the landless marrying between 1600 and 1624, on the other hand, the length of union is significantly briefer than for any other cohort. And although the childbearing span works out only marginally shorter than for 1560—99, it is over 3 years below that for 1625—49; while the average time elapsing between births is 2.5 months higher than for the preceding generation, and 5.0 months higher than for that which followed. Above all, the closed family size in the 1600—24 period is a mere 2.1 children, as against 3.0 for 1560—99 and 3.4 for 1625—49.

But can the inhibited fertility which has now been localized spatially, as it were, also be more tightly localized from the chronological point of view? Figure 13 plots the live conceptions of all identified landed and landless Solihull families whose years of potential childbearing ran

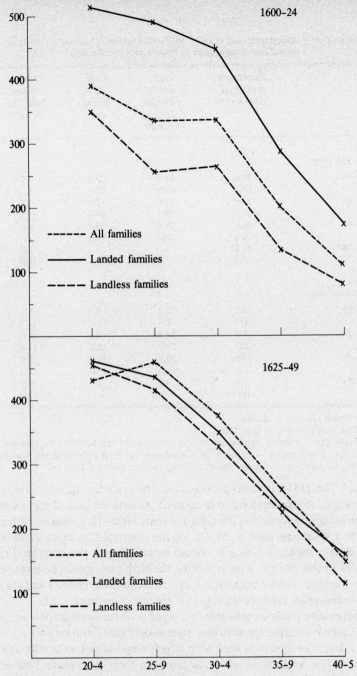

Fig. 12. Age-specific marital fertility in landed and landless families, 1600–49 – Sheldon, Solihull and Yardley (see Table III)

TABLE IV   *Demographic rates in landed and landless families, 1560–1674 – Sheldon,*
Solihull and Yardley (figure in brackets gives size of sample)

	Mean length of marriage union (years)	Mean birth intervals 1—4 (months)‡	Mean child-bearing span (years)‡	Mean closed family size (children)
Landed couples marrying				
1560—99	26.0	31.5	12.9	4.1
	(30)	(56)	(22)	(31)
1600—24	27.0	29.9	12.3	4.4
	(32)	(58)	(15)	(33)
1625—49	26.6	29.4	12.5	4.0
	(46)	(88)	(32)	(41)
1650—74*	21.1	—	—	3.8
	(53)			(56)
Landless couples marrying				
1560—99	26.3	32.4	8.9	3.0
	(17)	(29)	(15)	(21)
1600—24	17.0	34.9	8.8	2.1
	(25)	(30)	(12)	(26)
1625—49	20.8	29.9	12.0	3.4
	(16)	(31)	(14)	(19)
1650—74†	19.6	—	—	3.4
	(8)			(12)

*Paid hearth tax on 1 + hearths.
†Exempt from payment of hearth tax.
‡Normally these statistics depend on the use of completed families with 4+ children if female age of marriage is −30 and 6+ if it is unknown. Here, in order to secure workable samples, the analyses have been applied to closed families with 2 + children.

through the 1613—19 crisis period. Again the evidence, although statistically slight, is too emphatic to be ignored. Among the landed there were 13 live conceptions during the pre-crisis years 1600—12, giving an average of 1 to 2.8 woman-years lived. During the crisis itself 23 conceptions occurred at a mean of 1 to 2.6 woman-years. Prior to the crisis landless couples in this sample were matching the birth-rate of their betters with 16 conceptions in 45 woman-years, or 1 : 2.8. But between 1613 and 1619, 62 woman-years produce only 12 conceptions, a mean of 1 : 5.2.

Aggregative analysis, which is concerned with the demographic record of the whole community, provides more widely based support for the idea that a dearth of food may have been largely responsible for the difficulties of the 1610s. At Solihull where, as has been seen, conceptions between 1613 and 1617 were 26.3% down on the previous decade, the shortfall was particularly marked in the last quarter of the harvest year (Fig. 14), when

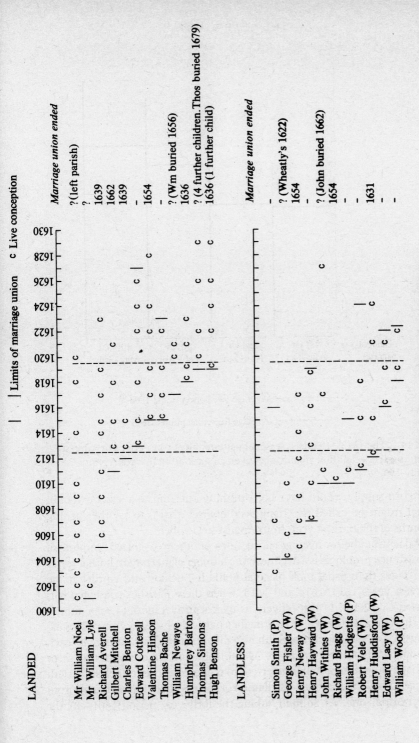

Fig. 13. The 1613—19 crisis: live conceptions in landed and landless families whose childbearing span ran through the crisis period, by harvest year — Solihull.

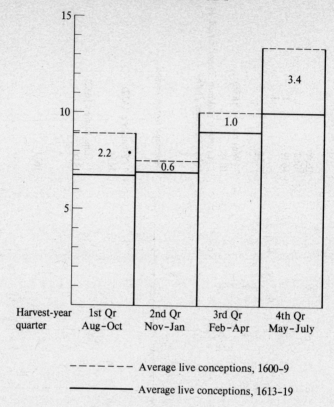

– – – – – – – Average live conceptions, 1600–9

———————— Average live conceptions, 1613–19

Fig. 14.   The 1613–19 crisis: seasonal pattern of live conceptions by harvest-year quarters – Solihull (figure gives average shortfall in live conceptions, 1613–19)

the corn supply would have been running out; and to a lesser extent in what might be called the 'hang-over' quarter, that is to say the opening months of the harvest year, from August to October.

Apart from below average conceptions, another recognized symptom of subsistence problems is a decline in the number of marriages. Rather fewer marriages than usual took place at Solihull, Sheldon and Yardley in the harvest years 1613, 1614 and 1615, when these parishes combined witnessed 13, 12 and 11 respectively, as against an average of 14.9 per annum for the 1610s. However, 1616 brought a particularly heavy crop of 22 weddings, 10 of which were at Solihull; while the three last crisis years each produced an annual total of 15. Overall, therefore, the crisis does not seem to have presented a major deterrent to matrimony. Nevertheless, as with conceptions, the seasonal distribution of events differed considerably from the normal one. At Solihull, taking the forty-year period 1601–40, the

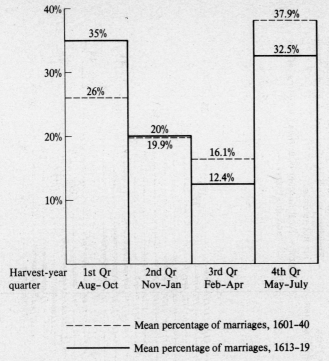

Fig. 15.   The 1613—19 crisis: seasonal pattern of marriages by harvest-year
quarters — Solihull

highest number of weddings took place in the last quarter of the harvest
year, May, June and July (Fig. 15). But if food was scarce the rump of the
harvest year would be no time for the poorer members of the community
at least to hold their wedding breakfast. And this presumably is why, during the years 1613—19, the fourth quarter, and to a lesser extent the third,
brought significantly fewer marriages than usual, while the quarter
immediately following the harvest tended to be oversubscribed. Of the 10
Solihull weddings taking place in the peak year of 1616, no less than 6
were solemnized in the first quarter: though, interestingly enough, these
do not seem to have been immediately productive. The same period was
among the lowest on record for conceptions. There were only 3, well below
half the first quarter mean for the crisis period itself, and only a third of the
corresponding figure for the previous decade.

Also suggestive of food shortage is the fact that 46% of adult burials during the crisis years were those of paupers. The rise in the number of such
burials is apparent from Figure 16; while Figure 17 shows that the level

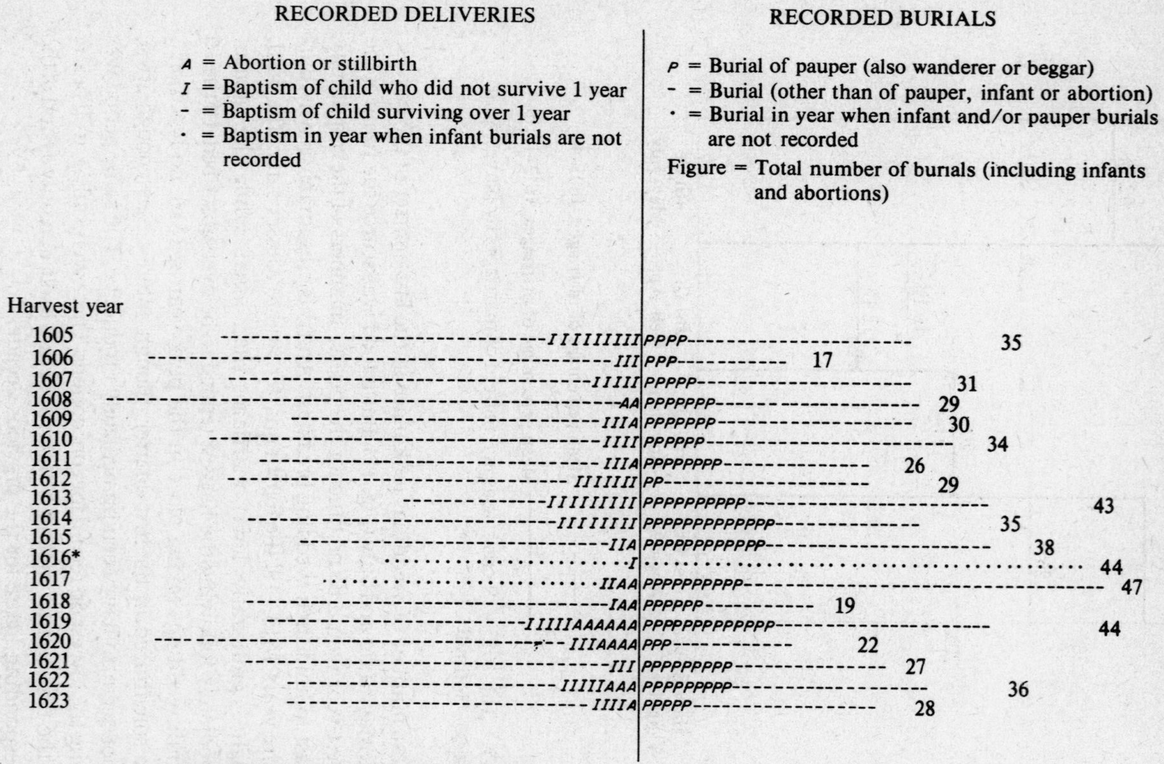

RECORDED DELIVERIES

RECORDED BURIALS

A = Abortion or stillbirth

I = Baptism of child who did not survive 1 year

- = Baptism of child surviving over 1 year

• = Baptism in year when infant burials are not recorded

P = Burial of pauper (also wanderer or beggar)

- = Burial (other than of pauper, infant or abortion)

• = Burial in year when infant and/or pauper burials are not recorded

Figure = Total number of burials (including infants and abortions)

Harvest year		
1605	----------------IIIIIIIIPPPP----	35
1606	-----------------III PPP----	17
1607	----------------IIIII PPPPP----	31
1608	---------------AA PPPPPPP----	29
1609	---------------IIIA PPPPPP----	30
1610	----------------IIII PPPPPP----	34
1611	---------------IIIA PPPPPPP----	26
1612	--------------IIIIIII PP----	29
1613	------------IIIIIIII PPPPPPP----	35
1614	------------IIIIIIII PPPPPPPPPP----	43
1615	------------IIA PPPPPPPPPP----	38
1616*	••••••••••••••••-I-••••••••••••••	44
1617	----------IIAA PPPPPPPP----	47
1618	-----------IAA PPPPP----	19
1619	----------IIIIIAAAAA PPPPPPPPPPP----	22
1620	•--IIIAAAA PPP----	27
1621	------------III PPPPPPPP----	36
1622	-----------IIIIIAAA PPPPPPPP----	28
1623	-----------IIIIA PPPP----	

*Categories of burials not particularized

Fig. 16.   The 1613—19 crisis: recorded deliveries and burials — Solihull

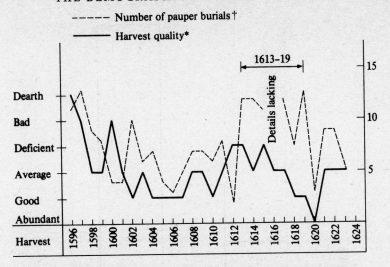

* See C. J. Harrison, 'Grain Price Analysis and Harvest Qualities, 1465-1634',
  Agricultural History Review, XIX, 1971, p. 154

†The first Solihull register records pauper burials only over the period 1596—1623.

Fig. 17.   Number of pauper burials related to harvest quality, 1596—1623 —
Solihull

which obtained virtually throughout the 1613—19 period had been
touched only once before: namely in the well-attested dearth of the 1590s.
And again, as with conceptions and marriages, the seasonal pattern
of pauper burials needs to be noted, 65% of them occurring in the
second half of the harvest year, with a particularly emphatic peak in the
third quarter (Fig. 18). Detailed investigations also show that a considerable number of paupers were relatively young, able-bodied men who in
normal circumstances would have been expected to manage without
parochial relief. Over the period 1596—1623 it is possible to establish the
age at death of 23 Solihull male paupers. Two were in their twenties, 5 in
their thirties, and 6 each in their forties and fifties. Moreover, 5 of the 19
'young' pauper burials which can be identified fall during the years 1596—
8, 8 during the years 1613—19. Apart from named paupers, other casual-
ties of the latter crisis have the look of people being pushed beyond
the limits of subsistence. To cite only one example, William Greswold
buried a chrisom child on 25 November 1613; a little daughter seven
months later, on 25 June 1614. On 30 July of the same year he himself is
buried.

Additional signs of subsistence difficulties which one may expect to find
in the burial records are an above average incidence of infant deaths and of

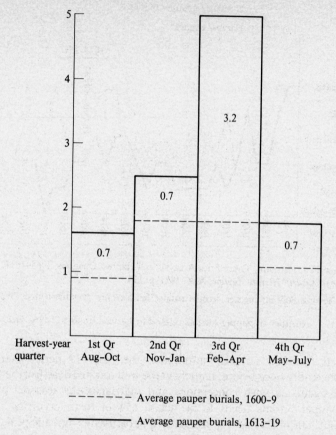

Fig. 18. The 1613–19 crisis: seasonal pattern of pauper burials by harvest-year quarters – Solihull (figure gives excess of pauper burials, 1613–19)

spontaneous abortions. Infant mortality was indeed high during the harvest years 1613 and 1614 (Fig. 16), when there are 17 infant burials at Solihull, as against 61 baptisms. This gives an infant mortality rate of about 280 per 1,000, as compared with an overall average for the first quarter of the seventeenth century of 148 per 1,000. Between December 1615 and August 1617 the register fails to distinguish infant burials, so it is impossible to say how many infant deaths occurred during the middle years of the crisis. However, one would have expected a comparison of the baptism and burial registers to bring to light the interment of baptized children who died under the age of one. The fact that it fails to do so, except in one or two cases, raises the possibility that the infant mortality rate may have been exceptionally low in the harvest years 1615 and 1616. Nor perhaps is this quite so surprising as at first it seems. For in these harsh times the families most likely to lose children in infancy would have been the poorer families. And, as has been shown, it was precisely such families that were giving birth to relatively few children.

Indeed, in 1615 and 1616, which represent the nadir of the crisis, the burials of no less than 19 Solihull wives are recorded, as against an average of only 3.7 per annum during the previous decade. This suggests that the birth-rate was perhaps being held back at this time not only because of a decline in fertility but also because actually or potentially expectant mothers were dying in unprecedented numbers. Of the 19 women concerned, 4 belonged to landed families. The others cannot be classified with certainty, but all except 2 or 3 bear surnames with pauper or cottager associations. Unfortunately none of their ages are known, and in only one case is the marriage recorded. On the other hand, 10 were childbearing during the 1600s and/or the early 1610s. At least 5 of these were probably still nubile, having borne children within the previous three years. A couple certainly were: for Joan Newway and Joan Worthen both died in childbirth — together with 2 probably nubile wives — in the August of 1616.

Even with the harvest years 1618 and 1619, when conceptions begin to pick up again, the infant mortality rate remains well below average. Now, however, we have a quite unprecedented spate of spontaneous abortions, culminating in 1 for every 5 live births in 1619 (Fig. 16).

It is as if, from the point of view of new life, the crisis passes through three distinct phases. In the two opening years poorer women are still bearing children, but a high proportion of their offspring are failing to survive infancy because of inadequate feeding. Then, at the heart of the crisis (1615—17), the food-base becomes so inadequate that many of the poorer women are unable to conceive at all. Finally, with its gradual abatement, they again begin to do so; but now, such is the backlog of malnutrition, as it were, that a significant proportion of them are unable to retain the foetus for a full term in the womb. It is interesting that this chronology ties in closely with that proposed by Professor McKeown. Discussing the influence of inadequate food supply on modern populations, he says 'Both experimental and clinical evidence suggest that the effect of such deficiencies is felt first on the newborn (leading to sickness or death), next on the probability of conception (through interruption of the sexual cycle) and last on pregnancy itself.'[8]

Figure 19 compares aspects of what might be called the mortality profile of the seven-year 1613—19 crisis at Solihull with that of the three-year 1596—8 dearth period in the same parish. When allowances are made for their different durations, the resemblances are considerable. In the 1590s, as in the 1610s, one finds the heaviest infant mortality at the beginning of

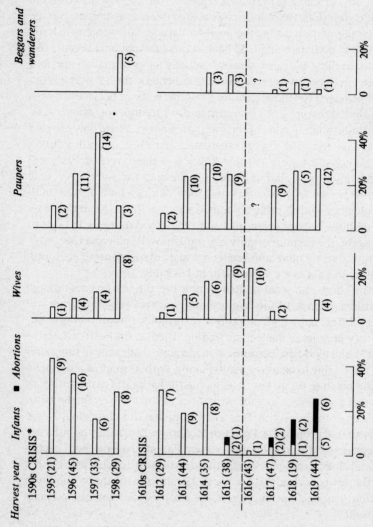

Fig. 19.   The 1590s and 1610s crises: pattern of 'sensitive' burials – Solihull – expressed as a percentage of annual burial totals (figure in brackets gives actual number).
*Nationally this crisis began in 1594, but it did not seriously affect north Arden until 1596 which brought the third successive dearth harvest.

the crisis; whereas among wives the mortality pattern is the reverse. The interment of considerable numbers of abortions may be a phenomenon which tends to be restricted to extremely sharp and lethal famine conditions, or to the latter years of a prolonged period of food deficiency. Certainly none appear to have taken place during the 1590s crisis: though it is possible that such burials did occur but went unrecorded. Finally, in both instances the crises are characterized by a steady build-up in the number of pauper burials, while after two or three years the deaths of wanderers, strangers and beggars are recorded: unfortunate people whose lives had been unhinged by the severities of the times, leaving them with no alternative but to take to the road, and ultimately to die on it.

Now such a sequence of demographic events is in fact readily understandable in the 1590s, when a succession of four bad seasons and disastrous harvests led to food shortage and crisis conditions in countless parishes throughout England. But what of the 1610s? According to the most recent study of harvest classifications, there was a run of three 'deficient', or slightly below par, barley harvests in the years 1612—14, and a 'bad' oats harvest followed in 1615. Moreover, barley and oats were the grains on which the poorer members of the community mainly depended (see p. 48). Nevertheless, overall, the 1613—19 period cannot be regarded as particularly unpropitious; and certainly there are no indications of dearth on the national, or even on the regional, scale. On the contrary, when all grains are taken into account, 5 of the 7 harvests in question are thought to have been of average quality or better and the other 2 only deficient (Fig. 17).[9] Yet locally the demographic record of these years is a great deal more alarming than that of the nationally recognized dearth. The 1596—8 crisis did indeed bring higher mortalities, with an average of 85 burials per annum in the five parishes, as against a mean of only 41 per annum in the previous decade. But we do not find a sustained shortfall in conceptions, such as occurred in 1613—17 (Fig. 20). Similarly, although burials soared during the midland dearth years of 1606—7, conceptions — the litmus of prolonged food shortage — appear to have been little affected. Indeed, they climb to a record of 112 in 1607, as against 78 burials. Since the 1613—19 crisis is so much more dearth-like than the recognized dearth periods, and since the seasons cannot be blamed, it seems difficult to avoid the conclusion that what we have in these north Arden parishes in the 1610s is a Malthusian situation at the local level. It looks as though resources, as they were at that time being exploited, were unable to support the ever growing population. Almost certainly, it was during this decade that Barnaby East and others, with the consent of the lord of the manor, 'plowed upp xiiii[th] acres or theire aboutes of the common or waste grounde of Yardeley for to sowe corne upon in this tyme of dearth'.[10]

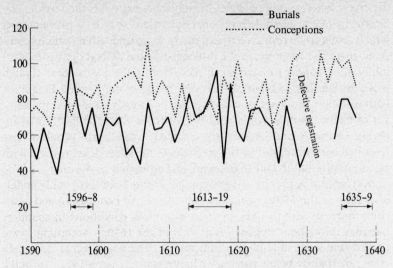

Fig. 20.   Burials and live conceptions by harvest year, 1590–1639 — Bickenhill, Sheldon, Solihull and Yardley

The term 'crisis of subsistence' is probably best avoided. In the classic
French instances such crises, which are always associated with widespread, rather than local, food shortage, show 'a sudden rise in burials,
double, or even treble the normal'.[11] Conceptions and marriages fall away
to a greater extent than is found in Arden, and some of the deaths are
known to have been due to starvation. Generally, too, if only because of
their extreme virulence, crises of subsistence tend to be of relatively short
duration, taking only one or two years to work their woe. The Arden crisis
is less vicious, but more persistent and prolonged. And indeed, this is as
one would expect if the cause of the trouble was not a sudden famine
bringing instant starvation but an endemic food shortage leading to creep-
ing malnutrition.

Although not of the same order as a crisis of subsistence, the 1613–19
malaise does appear to have been of the same kind. And as such, it may certainly be regarded as a mild Malthusian check, just as the crisis of subsistence may be regarded as a sharp and virulent one. As for the underlying
imbalance between population and resources of which the Malthusian
check was a manifestation, this is best described as a state of 'ecological
disequilibrium'.[12]

5

NEGATIVE RESPONSES

So far it has been argued that rapid demographic increase in the last quarter of the sixteenth century and early seventeenth century led to a state of 'ecological disequilibrium' in northern Arden, i.e., a serious imbalance between population and resources; and that, as a result, in the 1610s there was a mild Malthusian check on population growth. Immediately prior to this check the population of the five parishes had probably been somewhere in the region of 3,100. But the 'seven lean years' brought a reduction which was perhaps in the order of 10%. Certainly, the Cox estimate for the 1620s works out at 2,840, or over 8% below the analogous figure for the 1600s.[1] However, the fact that by 1640 the parishes had taken their combined total up to something like 3,400 — i.e., well beyond the pre-crisis figure — suggests that the underlying ecological difficulties must have been countered in some way. How then, did these Arden communities manage eventually to accommodate the extra numbers?

To begin with, certain negative responses can be isolated, through which the ecosystem was indicating, as it were, that such high numbers could not be supported. The first such response was of course the Malthusian check itself, as represented by the 1613–19 crisis. However, from the ecological point of view, and in a seventeenth-century context, this involuntary emetic may be regarded as having made its own contribution to the eventual solution. For, by significantly reducing numbers, it helped to trim the problem to size.

Secondly, as has already been shown, there was a considerable exodus of refugees from the ill-fated parishes in the 1610s, and this continued in the 1620s. Again, because emigration tended to dampen down population pressure, it may be regarded as a helpful negative response. A few of the families who disappear in the 1610s and 1620s, when the number of reproducing surnames is reduced from 453 to 384 (Fig. 4), may have died out during the crisis, but the majority are more likely to have emigrated. A study of the life histories of 200 children baptized at Solihull between 1601 and 1625 confirms that there were many departures. Fifty-four youngsters are thought to have left the parish with their parents, while a further 38 probably did so as individuals, rather than as part of a family unit. Taken together this means that 92 out of the 200 people concerned apparently emigrated before reaching the age of 29 — which may be regarded as approximating to the age of first marriage. Since 59 others were buried in the parish prior to reaching that age, it would seem that at most 1 in every 4 persons born at Solihull in this generation would have been represented by descendants here in its successor.

Among the migrants were many families who had only arrived in the 1600s. The Postans are first heard of in 1605 when a daughter, Alice, is baptized. A second daughter, Ursula, follows in 1608. But on 5 November 1612 Alice and Ursula are both buried, and on 12 July their mother, Anne. Foulke, the father, presumably moved off elsewhere — certainly nothing more is heard of him. Of the 11 foreigners whose place of origin is recorded in the parish register between 1599 and 1615 (Fig. 6), only 1 had connections in the parish a generation later. Three of the 4 who emanated from east of the River Avon had one event recorded against their name — a baptism — the other a baptism followed by an infant burial. Like the Postans, these families were unable to gain a foothold here. Having helped to produce the ecological imbalance by contributing to the abnormally high tide of immigration, they now to some extent helped to cure it, by departing.

Meanwhile, the parochial and manorial authorities were themselves actively discouraging immigration. In 1632 an enactment of the Solihull court leet forbade anyone to 'receive into his house any person other than a child or children without they give security that the parish shall not be burdened'; and John Miles forfeited 39s. 'because he received one William Lea' without doing so. Three others were fined in 1634 on a similar charge, and further cases are recorded in the 1640s. The 1613—19 crisis and the exodus which it precipitated were involuntary processes; this attempt to curb the settlement of foreigners represents a conscious negative response.

6

THE ECOLOGICAL PROBLEM

But negative responses, while they helped to contain the ecological problem, could not overcome it. If higher populations were to be supported, the local communities would have to react positively. To what extent, therefore, is it possible to interpret the economic changes which are known to have been taking place in the five parishes during the late Elizabethan and early Stuart period as positive responses to the ecological problem?

In a pre-industrial economy the most fundamental resource is land. Down to the mid sixteenth century it may be presumed that virtually all local households would have had a landholding in excess of 4 acres and were therefore able, to a greater or lesser extent, to provide for their own subsistence.

However, a population growth of over 800, such as occurred between the 1570s and the 1600s, would have involved the establishment of something in the order of 160 to 200 new households. In other woodland districts early agrarian development had often been inhibited by forest law, or alternatively large areas had reverted to waste during the late medieval contraction. But the Arden had seen extensive colonization in the thirteenth century and little long-term agrarian contraction thereafter, any abandoned acres being promptly added to the farms of the richer more thrustful peasantry. As a result the amount of unappropriated land available in the five parishes was strictly limited. It is estimated that c. 1550 there was about 2,260 acres of common waste in all — which represented under 9% of the total area.[1]

Despite this shortage of waste, there is a possibility that some attempt was at first made locally to implement the Elizabethan statute of 1589 which enacted that all new cottages must have at least 4 acres attached to them. Both at Solihull and Yardley the nineteenth-century enclosure maps show several intakes of about 4 acres at the edge or in the middle of areas of late surviving common. But a 4 acre policy — which would of course, as the act intended, have given new households some measure of independence — if ever espoused, must have been rapidly abandoned. The Survey of the Manor of Solihull made in 1606 refers to 'A cottage & five Acres and a halfe taken out of the Wast by Copy.' But the 7 cottages, hovels and shops listed in a similar document of 1581, and a further 5 cottages described as 'taken out of the Wast' in 1606 had only 'gardens, orchards, hemplecks, etc.' attached to them.

Far from all the newly formed households were accomodated on common land. Yeomen and husbandmen frequently let out portions of their holdings. Out of 75 tenements under 6 acres which are listed in the 1605 Knowle survey, at least 40 were sublettings of this kind. John Browne, a copyholder with 43 acres was renting out 4 cottages with small pieces of land attached. William Wheigham, who held about 20 acres, had two sub-tenants with 1 rood and 4 acres respectively. Forty-two of the 75 small tenements shared 91 acres of land between them, giving an average of 2.2 acres each. But 10 cottages had only 2–3 roods, while 23 had 1 rood or under. At Knowle itself all 'residents' could 'put any Beast, Sheep or any other Cattle' on the common.[2] However, the fact that all but 9 of the 42 tenants with 1 + acres devoted their holdings entirely to grass makes one wonder whether even those with a modicum of land — never mind the landless — were in fact regarded as residents. And certainly there is nothing to suggest that landless cottagers elsewhere enjoyed common grazing rights.

Such people were from the start in an entirely different category from the traditional inhabitant of Arden. Unlike the peasant or the long-established smallholder with 4 or 5 acres, the landless cottager could not even begin to provide his own subsistence. On the contrary, he would have no alternative but to purchase virtually all the food he required for himself and his family. And unfortunately the mid-sixteenth-century agrarian economy of these Arden parishes was not geared to produce the kind of food he could afford. The basic food of the poor had always been bread and cheese — or rather 'whitsul', which Richard Carew, writing of Cornwall in the early seventeenth century, described as 'milk, sour milk, cheese, butter, and such like as came from the cow and ewe'.[3] But in the mid sixteenth century local farmers were growing only enough corn to satisfy their own requirements; and, although there was some dairying, their main surplus product was beef cattle, which presumably they sent on the hoof to distant markets.

Bearing this starting point in mind, we can now look at agrarian developments from the 1570s onwards to see if they did anything to improve the local food-base by making available the specific foodstuffs which so many of the newly formed households must have required.

7

POSITIVE RESPONSES: AGRARIAN CHANGE

A detailed discussion of agrarian change, based on the analysis of 217 probate inventories by forty-year periods (1530–69, 1570–1609 and 1610–49), has been published elsewhere.[1] The most fundamental development was a shift in the balance between pasture and arable. However, this adjustment in primary land use did not take place until after 1610. In the period 1530–69 only about a third of the land was being used for the growing of arable crops, about two-thirds being pasture. The same traditional land-use pattern persisted during the forty years 1570–1609 — i.e., the period which has now been identified as one of steady population build-up

(Table V and Fig. 21). But then, in the period 1610—49 — or in other words, the period which accompanied and followed the 1613—19 crisis — the arable/pasture ratio is adjusted to roughly 50:50. Over the previous eighty years crops had accounted for only 17 or 18% of the total farm value: now there is a rise to 31%.[2] This mounting interest in arable cultivation is shared by all categories of farmer, from the 60—100 acre yeoman down to the lesser husbandman with 10—15 acres. At the same time, it is the big farmer who is most committed to the new trend, his crop value advancing from 16.8% of the appraised produce (including draught animals) to 37.4%, as compared with the small peasant's movement from 14.2 to 23.3%.[3] Moreover, this proves to be the establishment of a long-term trend. By the period 1650—89 the arable/pasture ratio has moved to 60:40.

One way in which the arable may have been increased is suggested by Edmund Gibson in the notes to his 1695 edition of Camden's *Britannia*. Speaking of Arden, he says that 'the Iron-works in the Counties round, destroy'd such prodigious quantities of wood, that they quickly lay the Country a little open, and by degrees made room for the plough'.[4] Local documentation confirms this statement to some extent. At Knowle in 1605 there were 7,000 oaks and 100 ash trees 'growing in the woods of the demesne and in the waste of the . . . manor', of which 2,000 oaks were reserved 'for timbering'. John Cope, Esq., had 'thrown to the ground forty better oaks', and Fulk Grevill had cut down others, 'by what right' the jurors did not know. John Hugford in the same year had 300 oak trees on his farm, including 6 which had been cut for timber, while there were also 8 (felled?) ash trees, plus 152 cartloads of firewood. Such men may well have been sending 'prodigious quantities of wood' to 'the Iron-works in the Counties round'. Certainly there was considerable interest in the clearing of demesne woodland by the middle years of the seventeenth century. At nearby Hampton-in-Arden in 1649 'woods standing and growing' which 'may at present be disposed of' are valued at £572.[5] The vendors of Forshaw manor (a sub-manor of Solihull) in 1652 envisaged the reclamation of 120 acres of 'Coppice wood', specifying the value of 'The trees & other woods now growing' (£151), and what 'the soyle there will be worth to be letten p. annum . . . when cleared of the trees & underwood.'[6] There is also some evidence for the reclamation of waste land. Apart from cottagers who are constantly trying to minimize their landlessness by adding small, surreptitious encroachments to their holdings, we read of 'five closes called le Waste' at Knowle in 1605, while a sizable portion of Bickenhill Heath was enclosed in 1614.[7]

But despite this, the amount of wood and heath brought into cultivation must have been relatively minimal. A much more important factor in accounting for the extension of the arable acreage was the introduction

TABLE V Model farm economy, 1530–1689 (based on summer inventories)

	1530–69 22 inventories	1570–1609 13 inventories	1610–49 19 inventories	1650–89 21 inventories
Mean acreage of winter corn per farm	3.2	1.5	3.3	6.8
Mean acreage of spring corn per farm	2.8	1.8	5.5	8.9
Mean acreage of unspecified corn per farm	0.5	2.7	2.4	3.4
Mean sown acreage per farm	6.6	6.0	11.2	19.1
Estimated fallow acreage per farm	3.3	3.0	5.6	9.5
Mean total arable acreage per farm	9.9	9.0	16.8	28.6
Mean number of cattle per farm	18.1	14.3	12.2	13.8
Mean number of horses per farm	2.5	1.6	2.0	4.1
Mean number of sheep per farm	10.6	15.0	20.6	8.1
Mean number of pigs per farm	5.1	4.9	2.3	2.8
Estimated grass acreage per farm	22.7	18.9	18.3	19.5
Estimated mean total acreage per farm	32.6	27.9	35.1	48.1
Estimated arable/pasture ratio	30:70	32:68	48:52	59:41

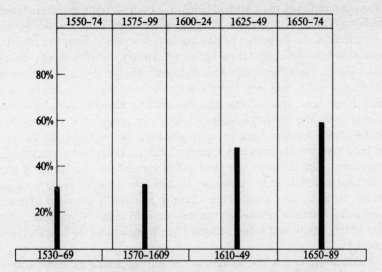

Fig. 21.   Proportion of land used as arable, 1530—1689 (see Table V)

into the Arden area of up-and-down or convertible husbandry. Early-seventeenth-century deeds frequently speak of 'a close of arable or pasture', which presumably refers to this convertible, up-and-down land. Similarly there are many instances of the division of the formerly large pasture closes into parts, so that the new temporary tillages could be rotated. The Knowle survey (1605) mentions 'Two closes of pasture now divided into three, near Bentley Heath'; the 1632 Solihull survey 'a parcel of land ... late William Colmores ... now into two parts divided', etc. At Church Bickenhill in 1649 'one close of pasture ground called the Castle Hills' was 'devided into seaven parts, whereof some parte thereof is att present plowed, it being the usuall course thereabouts soe to doe'.[8]

Other improvements accompanied the introduction of convertible husbandry. References to marling are particularly numerous during the early seventeenth century, and in 1667 the inventory of Richard Bache of Solihull lists 'One load of Lyme and earth meaned together to lay on for barley.'[9] There was also intensive enclosure activity. The Bickenhill enclosure of 1614, which has already been referred to, was effected by a tripartite indenture made between Sir Robert ffysher, Thomas Wall, yeoman, and Hugh Large, husbandman, As well as enclosing 'parte of Bicknell heathe' with 'stakes postes and rayles', it brought 'convenyentlye together' the three parties' 'landes and groundes lying within the Common ffyeldes of Hill and Myddle Bicknell', the total area involved probably amounting to about 300 acres. By 1677, 137 out of 322 acres belonging to the Fisher and

Cousens families in the common fields of Church Bickenhill were enclosed. Although direct evidence is lacking, considerable areas of Marston Wavers and Elmdon are suspected of passing into severalty during the late six-teenth and the first half of the seventeenth century, the movement perhaps reaching its peak between 1620 and 1660. The principal instigators at Bickenhill were probably the Fishers as manorial lords; and the same may have been true at Marston Wavers and Elmdon, both of which belonged to the thrustful Maine family. But progressive yeomen and husbandmen seem to have been equally keen on enclosure. At Yardley in 1642 William Marston had 'fourteen lands . . . lately inclosed and lying together . . . in the common field called Heynefield'. But there is still 'one land or selion of the customary land of John Flynt . . . lying amongst them'. In order to complete his severalty Marston is prepared to grant 'two other lands or selions within the said field called Heynefield . . . for and in lieu of the said selion of John Flynt lying among the said fourteen lands'.[10]

Marling improved the fertility of the soil; enclosure gave the farmer greater control over his land; above all, convertible husbandry, by 'taking the plough round the farm', could result in the doubling of arable yields, as well as an analogous improvement of grazing on the new 'lays' of 'Fifteen or Twenty yeares'. There can be little doubt that the overriding objective in all this was to increase corn production as a means of increas-ing profits. And indeed, that is what the local market situation must have been encouraging farmers to do. Between the 1540s and the 1640s the national price index of animal products went up threefold; that of corn fourfold.[11] If anything, the local differential is likely to have been even greater. We know that corn was in short supply in the Arden area during 1587. In the *Book of John Fisher* full details are given of grain coming into and out of the Warwick market during that dearth year. Over the peak period in November and December an average of 400 bushels per week was changing hands, most of it being sold by farmers and bodgers from the Feldon and purchased by men from Arden. The two most corn-hungry places were the neighbouring parishes of Tanworth-in-Arden and Solihull, the latter having as many as six different traders at Warwick during the one year.[12] Nor does this scarcity seem to have been exceptional, merely a dearth phenomenon. Rather it looks as if it may have been perennial and chronic. For, whereas the local price index for cattle was marginally below the national index over the period 1590–1649, the index for arable crops was on average 13% above the national figure (Fig. 22). In these circum-stances, the adoption of convertible husbandry and the accompanying improvements could hardly fail to commend themselves.

Nevertheless, early-seventeenth-century farmers could have been grow-

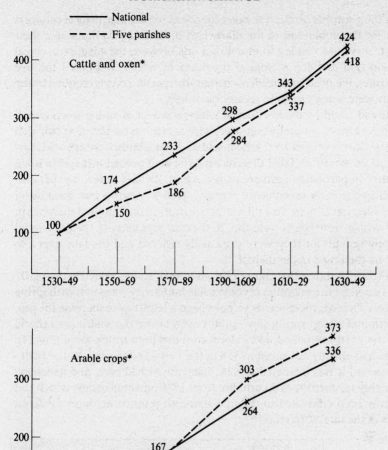

Fig. 22.   Local and national price indices, 1530—1649

*Local indices for cattle and oxen, and for the arable crops (price per acre) are
derived from probate inventories, which, although wayward in their valuation
of domestic goods, are clearly sensitive to price movements of agricultural
produce. Both national indices are based on Thirsk, *Agrarian History of England
and Wales*, IV: cattle and oxen, p.858, arable crops, p.857.

ing their surplus corn not to meet the consumer demand of local cottagers
but for the upper end of the market, as indeed they had produced their
beef. If we are seeking to establish a link between the advance in cereal
production and the ecological predicament which confronted the five
parishes, we need to consider whether the specific cereals required by the
poor were being grown in greater quantities.

Bread could be made either of winter-sown or of spring-sown grains.
But the former generally cost over twice as much as the latter. At Norwich
in the dearth year of 1597 wheat sold at 7s. 0d. a bushel, rye at 6s. 4d., barley at 2s. 9d. to 3s. 0d.[13] Clearly what the poor needed was spring-sown
grains: in particular, perhaps, barley. Again, Richard Carew says of Cornwall in the early seventeenth century, 'Barley is grown into great use of
late years, so as now they till a larger quantity in one hundred than was in
the whole shire before; and this, in the dear seasons past, the poor found
happy benefit, for they were principally relieved and the labourers also
fed by the bread made thereof.'[14]

Figure 23 shows that most of the additional arable created in the 1610—
49 period by the adoption of convertible husbandry was sown with spring
grains. Indeed, there seems to have been a tendency to increase the production of cheap spring-sown grains even before the Malthusian check.
In the 1530—69 period 45% of local corn had been spring-sown (Fig. 24).
This had already advanced to 53% in the 1570—1609 period. By the 1610—
49 period it has increased to 62%. Oats always had been, and remained,
a highly favoured spring corn. But from 1570 onwards barley, which had
hardly been cultivated in the mid sixteenth century, accounts for about
20% of the total corn crop.[15]

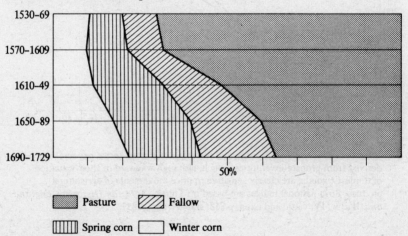

Fig. 23.   Land use, 1530—1729 (based on summer inventories) (see Table V)

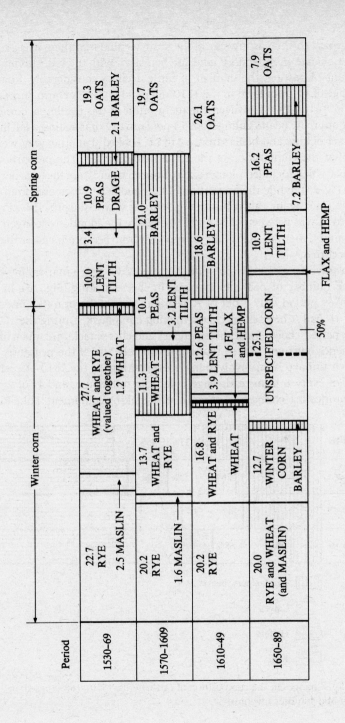

Fig. 24. Changes in the proportion of arable crops, 1530–1689 (based on summer inventories)

Turning to the pasture side of the farm, we find that there was a significant change in secondary land use here also. With the reduction in the amount of pasture, the number of cattle declines considerably, from an average of 14.1 per farm in the 1530—69 period to 8.6 per farm during the period 1610—49.[16] However, the main brunt of this decline is borne by meat animals: beasts falling from 5.1 per farm to 2.0, as against a fall in the number of kine and heifers from 6.4 to 5.0. Looked at another way, we can say that the composition of the cattle herd changed. The proportion of beasts (which included plough oxen) dropped from 37% of the total herd to 24% (Fig. 25); while the proportion of kine and heifers increased from 45% to 59%. And again, this adjustment got under way in the pre-crisis period. Indeed, it was between 1570 and 1609, before the adoption of convertible husbandry, that the main shift of emphasis from beef production to dairying occurred.

Meanwhile, alongside these developments, we find a marked increase in the number of peasants involved in cheese-making (Fig. 26). In the 1530—69 period only 3 out of 70 peasants had a dairy or milkhouse and only 16 had 'Cheysses' or cheese-making equipment. During the 1570—1609 period cheese vats, cheese presses and cheese racks are much more frequently encountered, so that approximately 50% of the peasantry are known to have been involved in cheese-making. By the 1610—49 period I out of every 6 farmsteads have a dairy or milkhouse; and 41 of the 68 inventories list cheeses, 14 others cheese-making equipment. Luke Rider

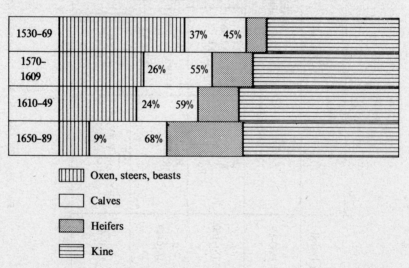

Fig. 25. Changes in the composition of cattle herds, 1530—1689 (based on winter and summer inventories)

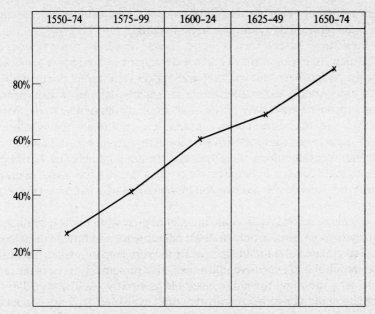

| 1550–74 | 1575–99 | 1600–24 | 1625–49 | 1650–74 |

Fig. 26. Percentage of inventoried households with cheese and/or cheese-making equipment, 1550–1674

of Solihull (1630) has 'Cheese in the house ... £10'; Robert Harrison of Sheldon (1645) 'one hundred weight of cheese'. In twelve other cases the 'greate', 'small', or 'softe' cheeses (sometimes coupled with butter) are valued at £1 or over.[17]

Incidentally, it is somewhat surprising that, although bacon was the recognized meat of the poor, the number of pigs drops, alongside beef cattle, from an average of 4.1 per farm in the 1530–69 period to a mere 1.5 in the period 1610–49. The clearance of oak woodland and consequent reduction in the supply of acorns may be partly responsible. But bearing in mind Richard Carew's definition of 'whitsul', it is also possible that the waste dairy products, the whey and skimmed milk, once used as pig food, was later sold to the poor.

We are now in a position to see that the agrarian changes of the late Elizabethan and early Stuart period must indeed have had the effect of improving the local food-base, and may therefore be thought of as a positive response to the area's ecological problem. The population build-up, and with it the build-up of landless cottagers, was well under way from 1570 onwards. In response, we find, already in the 1570–1609 period, long before the demographic crisis, that local farmers are beginning to grow rather more spring-sown grain, particularly barley. And simultaneously they begin tapering down their meat production in order to concentrate more on dairying and cheese-making.

Both these adaptations, we must assume, would be made not out of Christian charity or altruism but in self interest and in response to market forces. As has been shown, local grain prices were exceptionally high at this time. And for the smaller farmer particularly, dairying, with its steady daily income, would have provided an attractive alternative to the extremely long-term business of meat production — it took four years before a beef animal was ready to be driven to some distant market. And aside from business considerations, there was also the unmistakable fact that when the cottager became a charge on the parish — as we know all too many of them did — it was the yeoman and husbandman who had to pay the poor rate.

Changing secondary land use in order to provide more cheap grain and whitsul would involve only minimal adjustments, and little in the way of capital outlay. Substantially increasing the corn crop necessitated a much more radical and expensive adjustment. That presumably is one of the reasons why the move towards convertible husbandry — and also enclosure activity — did not gather momentum until after 1600. Expensive innovation of this kind would not have seemed worth risking until it was perfectly certain that the demand for corn was there.

So the agrarian response is best seen as taking place in two phases: (1) adjustments in secondary land use; and (2) adjustments in primary land use, once the viability of the new market situation had been established (Fig. 27).

Perhaps the wealthy Solihull severalty farmer, Robert Palmer, who died in June 1649, best epitomizes these early-seventeenth-century agrarian developments at their point of completion. On a farm of about 80 acres, he had 34 acres of growing corn. Roughly 75% of this was spring-sown, namely: 'eight dayes worke of Barley ... sixteene dayes work of oats and two dayes work of pease'. Against this, there was only 'eight dayes works of wheate and Ry', which was presumably for home consumption. Including 'Corn in the Barne unthresht' from the previous year (£6 6s. 8d.), the total crop value comes to £56 6s. 8d. On the pasture side of the farm, which, making an allowance for common grazing, probably amounted to about 30 acres, Robert Palmer kept 'eight Cowes and one Bull', 'five two year old heifers', and 'six weaning calves'. Apart from a plough-team of six oxen, there were no beasts. His farmstead had a day house', which was equipped with 'a Churne', 'a skimmer', 'a cheese presse'; and a chamber in the house contained 'Certain cheese' worth about £2. Clearly, Robert Palmer, and his like, had moved with the times.

But if from as early as the 1570—1609 period local farmers were begin-

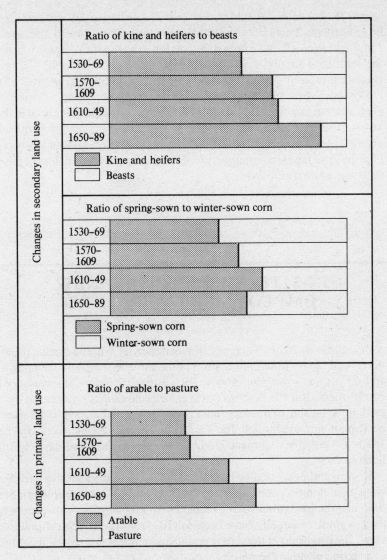

Fig. 27.   Changes in secondary and primary land use, 1530–1689 (based on inventories)

ning to produce the cheap foods required by the poor, why did the 1613–19 crisis occur at all? The fact that the serious national dearth of the 1590s was relatively mild here may mean that down to that point the supply of cheap foods had more or less kept pace with the rise in numbers. But the unprecedented influx of immigrants in the 1600s must greatly have intensified the ecological difficulties. Had convertible husbandry and the other improvements been fully established by this time, instead of merely coming in, it might have been different. But as it was, the possibility is that the local food supply — and in particular the local corn supply — simply was not increased quickly enough to feed all the additional mouths.

However, there may have been another contributory factor of equal, or even greater, importance. It is more than likely that some of the poor in the 1610s would not have been able to buy a sufficiency of bread and whitsul, even if enough had been available. The provision of cheap food answered only half the landless cottagers' problem. If they were to pay for the food, they also needed employment.

8

POSITIVE RESPONSES: NEW EMPLOYMENT OPENINGS

A peasant with 10 or 15 acres of land can manage without buying provisions; and, apart from finding his rent, he can also manage — at a pinch, and for a time — without money. Such a man, therefore, does not need employment. But the landless cottager, since he cannot produce his own food, must be able to produce money; which means that, poor relief aside, he cannot support himself and his family without getting work. In the 1610s it is possible that many landless cottagers found it inordinately difficult to do so.

However, the fact that by the mid seventeenth century the five parishes were managing to accommodate a sizable body of such people implies that, like the food problem, the employment problem — to some extent at least — must eventually have been solved. From the ecological point of view, the provision of these new employment openings may be regarded as a second positive response.

The agrarian changes would themselves have helped to create additional work. Dairying is more labour-intensive than beef production; and so is arable cultivation. 'There are no two trades', says Carew, 'which set so many hands on work at all times of the year as that one of tillage.'[1] In 1550 a correspondent of William Cecil's wrote 'owte of the dekaye of tyllage spryngethe ii evylls, skarsyte of korne and the pepull unwroughte'.[2] It follows that from the advance of tillage must have sprung two goods: an increase of corn and an increase of employment.

In absolute terms, an extension of arable from a third to a half of the total farm land would represent an increase of about 3,700 acres over the five parishes as a whole. On small farms the husbandman himself would be able to cope with the extra labour involved. But rather more than half the land was held in units of 30 + acres. So, as a result of the introduction of convertible husbandry, perhaps something like 2,000 additional acres would have had to be cultivated by farm servants. Allowing, say, one labourer for every 20 acres, this would provide full-time employment for perhaps 100 landless householders. At Knowle, in 1660, 76 out of 229 males paying the poll tax were employed as agricultural labourers or men servants. This represented 33% of adult males, as against 27% who were farmers.[3] So there was an average of 1.2 farm labourers per farm. And in addition, of course, arable land would have provided a great deal more casual work for women and children than pasture: stone-picking, bird-scaring, weeding and, above all, harvesting.

However, since local farmers were not beginning to adopt convertible husbandry on any scale until after 1600, the benefits of the advance of arable, from the point of view of employment, no less than of food supply, would only have become operative after the 1613—19 crisis. In the pre-crisis period the 'ii evylls' of inadequate tillage — 'the pepull unwroughte', no less than 'skarsyte of korne' — would both have applied. The fact that they did not both apply thereafter — or not to the same extent — may mean that the introduction of convertible husbandry made as great a contribution to the solving of the area's ecological problem as any other single factor.

But agriculture by itself could not provide enough work to give all the landless householders and their families adequate employment. A considerable proportion must have got their living by following some form of industrial pursuit.

Woodland crafts had been practised in north Arden from early medieval times. In the main, they derived either from the natural resources of the area — carpentry, coopery, tile-making — or from the locally produced raw materials of its pastoral economy — tanning and weaving.

Unfortunately, our knowledge of industrial employment depends largely on chance references to craftsmen in parish registers (the Yardley P. R. gives some occupations, 1600—17; Solihull, 1603—20), deeds, Quarter Sessions records, etc. Inventories can provide useful insights into the circumstances of individual craftsmen, but are too infrequent for systematic analysis. At Solihull from 1605 onwards a 'Mr. Thomas Wheatly's dole' was distributed annually to 'four decayed tradesmen'. But it is not until 1650 that the trades of recipients are listed.[4] Because of the patchy nature of the evidence it is impossible to establish a precise chronology for most industrial developments; or — except at Knowle in 1660, when the poll tax provides a full occupational structure — to make a reliable assessment of the proportion of inhabitants engaged in the various industrial pursuits.[5] Figure 28, which plots the number of named craftsmen occurring in the five parishes in the periods 1530—89 and 1590—1649, and receiving Wheatly's dole between 1650 and 1719, should therefore be regarded as, at best, giving a general idea of what was happening. Certainly, since it is not even comparing like with like, it has no absolute numerical validity.

Without question, however, the number of craftsmen did increase very considerably during the period under review. Furthermore, whereas all but a few of those working in the 1530—89 period would have been farmer or smallholder craftsmen, following their trade merely as part-time by-employment, the vast majority of those occurring from 1590 onwards were landless craftsmen, engaged in full-time industrial activity.

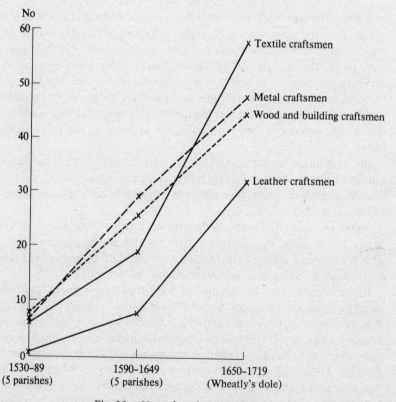

Fig. 28.   Named craftsmen, 1530—1719

All the medieval crafts of the area persisted and developed. Tanning had been, and remained, an enterprise run by farmer craftsmen, though the 9 decayed tanners who received Wheatly's dole, 1650—1719, were doubtless wage-earners employed at one of the area's Tanyard Farms. The secondary leather crafts of shoe-making and glove-making, on the other hand, were relatively easy crafts for the landless cottager to take up on his own account, for they required only a small capital outlay. The earliest known shoe-maker (John Pynyng of Solihull, d. 1535) followed his calling with nothing more than 'a whetstone, a parying knife & a shaping knife, the lasts & all other shop stuff' — valued at 2s. 8d. Although no glovers and only 2 shoe-makers occur in the 1590—1649 period, 7 of the former and 16 of the latter are listed among the recipients of Wheatly's dole.

Like tanning, weaving had been present from the fourteenth century onwards, though it collects only very occasional references until the 1590—1649 period, when 14 weavers have been traced in the five parishes. By the mid seventeenth century it had probably become the strongest single industrial pursuit, for no less than 31 weavers receive Wheatly's dole; while at Knowle in 1660 25, or 11%, of adult males follow the same occupation.

But the effect which weaving had on the employment situation in the area must have been even greater than these figures suggest. For this craft did more than provide work and earnings for the full-time weavers themselves. Since it took a quite disproportionate amount of labour to keep one weaver supplied with yarn, it also generated what was easily the area's most important domestic by-employment.

The lengthy and time-consuming process through which hemp or flax had to pass before it was ready for the loom can be deduced from probate inventories. After harvesting and drying, it had to be threshed, then retted for 7 to 20 days in water. Next came 'dressing', which involved two separate processes, 'breaking' and 'hatchelling'. Finally, the fibres had to be combed into 'slippings' of loose, untwisted yarn, before being spun on 'little wheels' into the finished thread. Two full-time 'hatchelors' occur at Knowle in 1660, but in the main such work was done by the women and children of small husbandmen and cottagers.

To some extent it is possible to document the growth of this absolutely vital cottage industry, and to see how it relates chronologically to the population build-up. The proportion of households of below average wealth in which carding and spinning equipment is found increases with particular sharpness during the late sixteenth century (Fig. 29). Of greater significance, perhaps, is the fact that, from the 1600—24 generation — but not before — we begin to come across hemp and flax among the growing crops listed in inventories. By the 1625—49 post-crisis period,

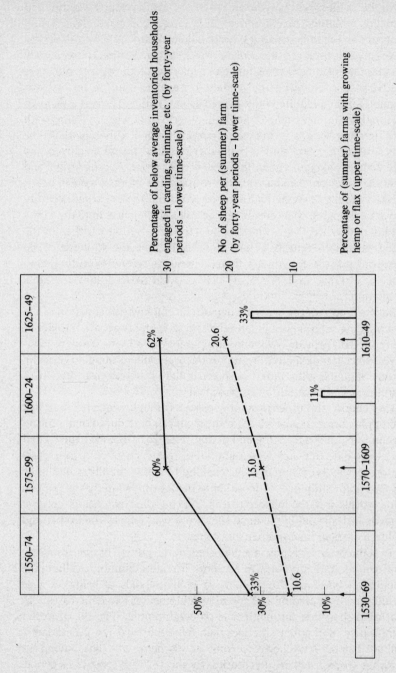

Percentage of below average inventoried households engaged in carding, spinning, etc. (by forty-year periods – lower time-scale)

No of sheep per (summer) farm (by forty-year periods – lower time-scale)

Percentage of (summer) farms with growing hemp or flax (upper time-scale)

Fig. 29.   Evidence relating to textile manufacture, 1550–1649 (based on inventories)

indeed, 1 in every 3 farmers is cultivating one or the other. The quantities involved were small — usually only a half to one acre. However, one enterprising Yardley farmer is known to have sown 22 acres with flax in 1634. Because the crop, which was valued at £50, was so unusual, there was a tithe dispute about it.[6] In any case, as far as providing work was concerned, a little flax or hemp apparently went a long way. In James I's reign a Gloucestershire farmer planted 40 acres 'and claimed to employ eight hundred people in cultivating and dressing it'.[7]

Of course, if the landless cottager could grow his own flax or hemp, that was still better. A few appear to have done this on their small plots of ground in preference to growing vegetables. The 1 bay cottage which Christopher Perse was renting at Knowle in 1605 had only 1 rood of land attached. But he was using this not as garden — he had only a 'backside' — but as 'hempland'. Another cottager, John Browne, had divided his 2 roods of ground between 'hempland' and garden.[8]

There can be no doubt that farmers were responding to the resource needs of an expanding textile industry in taking up the cultivation of hemp and flax. Several factors may have contributed to the substantial growth in the size of sheep flocks (Fig. 29); but the ever increasing demand for wool on the part of local weavers would almost certainly have been one of them.

The ubiquitous smiths aside, there are no references to the metal trades in the five parishes during the early medieval period. But by the beginning of the sixteenth century iron workers were spreading throughout the Birmingham district. In 1507/8 we come across Nicholas Coterel of Yardley, flecher (maker of arrows), and Thomas Pratty of Yardley, whirler (wiredrawer). Another whirler, Thomas Jeffrey is found in 1539. Edmund Underhill, a scythesmith who died in 1538, seems to have been in business in a particularly big way. Appended to his will is a list of monies due to him 'for sythes', his debtors including men not only from King's Norton and Birmingham but from places as far afield as Fillongley, Hill Morton (near Rugby) and Bridgnorth.[9]

The metal trades differed from all other local crafts in one important respect. The basic raw materials were not indigenous; they had to be brought into the parishes from Birmingham and the Black Country. Iron and coal were being extracted at Sedgeley and Walsall as early as the thirteenth century, but the quantity of iron smelted remained minimal throughout the Middle Ages. However, the early Tudor period brought an expansion of primary production, and since timber was already becoming scarce in the Black Country itself, the industry began to spread into new areas, including Handsworth and Perry Barr in the middle Tame valley to the north of Birmingham. Towards the end of the sixteenth century, this geographical extension was further encouraged by the advent of a new two-stage technology for producing wrought iron, based on the blast furnace and the finery forge, instead of the primitive medieval bloomery. Since the recapitalized industry operated on a much bigger scale than before, even greater quantities of charcoal were needed; and it may have been the exhaustion of charcoal supplies from the Handsworth and Perry woods that led to the opening, by 1615, of Aston Furnace, which was perhaps specifically sited 'to be within reach of the wooded Arden country'.[10]

It is likely enough that local wood and charcoal — there were two charcoal burners working at Bickenhill in the 1630s — would have been supplied to Aston Furnace from this time onwards; and certainly, the eastward migration of the iron industry brought our parishes more within its reach than they had been before. Nevertheless, during the first four decades of the seventeenth century specialized metal workers remained confined to the westernmost of the five parishes, Yardley (Fig. 30). Not until 1645 and 1648 do we come across the first metal craftsmen — apart from blacksmiths — at Sheldon and Solihull respectively, while they are even later reaching Bickenhill and Knowle. Incidentally, there appears to have been a parallel and — since metal workers used coal industrially — no doubt related delay in the introduction of coal (Fig. 31). This was being used in domestic hearths at Yardley from the early 1610s but does not reach Solihull until a generation later.

Most of the metal trades were not excessively demanding in terms of capital requirements. Symon Rotton, a landless cutler of Yardley (d. 1634), had £2 3s. out of his total estate of £9 7s. 10d. tied up in the equipment of

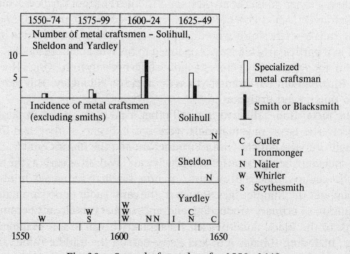

Fig. 30.   Spread of metal crafts, 1550–1649

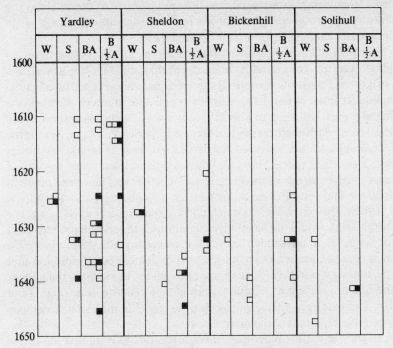

■ Inventories specifying coal or coal hatchet, scuttle, etc.

□ Inventories specifying grate(s) (but not coal, etc.)

W = Wealthy (Above twice average estate)

S = Substantial (Average – twice average estate)

BA = Below Average (Average – $\frac{1}{2}$ average estate)

B$\frac{1}{2}$A = Below half average estate

Fig. 31.   Incidence of coal and grates 1600–49 (based on inventories)

his 'shoppe', which included 'one paire of bellows, one handfeld, one gla-
sier, one Cutlers saw, one iron grate, one fyle and one draweing knyffe'.
Robert Harrison, a Sheldon nailer (d. 1645), managed with 'one payre of
bellowes & other naylors tools' valued at £1. As far as raw materials are
concerned, some metal workers were doubtless receiving them through
the putting-out system, which is known to have been developing in the
local iron industry at this time.[11] William Bysell of Yardley, who died in
1626, seems to have been functioning as an ironmonger-farmer: his inventory lists 'iron warre and coffers to laye it in, shoope tooles, weights beame
and schales'. The trade apparently persisted in the family, for a century
later (c. 1730) a George Bissell is described as an ironmonger in a Yardley
tithe dispute.[12] One of the deponents testifies 'that he often uses his own

team in carrying his own goods and in fetching iron from Birmingham and in carrying iron goods to several places for sale and uses the same team in husbandry as much as he does in the said trade'.

The tally of known Yardley metal workers in the first half of the seventeenth century consists of 2 cutlers, 3 whirlers and 3 nailers, as well as a 'striker' and 8 smiths, most of whom were probably engaged in industrial manufacturing, rather than, or as well as, general smithery. Although the metal trades had been so slow in reaching Solihull, by the second half of the seventeenth century they had become extremely common. Among the 'decayed tradesmen', 1650—1719, were 26 nailers, 11 smiths, 2 whirlers and 2 cutlers. In fact, 24% of all Wheatly dole recipients over this period were engaged in one of the metal trades. On the other hand, at Knowle in 1660 we find only 1 nailer, 1 'metelman', 1 ironmonger and 4 smiths.

Unless the available documentation is particularly misleading, the metal trades would not have helped significantly in providing employment for landless cottagers much before 1650, except at Yardley. Here, however, their contribution is likely to have been considerable, both before and after the 1613—19 crisis. This parish, indeed, suffered less sharply than any of the others — except Bickenhill — during the seven lean years (Figs. 9 and 10); and readily available employment openings in the metal trades may well have been part of the reason.

In the age of the timber-framed house the 'Great Rebuilding' must have given a major boost to the woodwork trades. During mid Tudor times 86% of the inventoried peasantry had lived in a house of three rooms or less (Fig. 32). By the second generation of the seventeenth century 64% lived in a house of six rooms or more. Figure 33, which shows the mean house

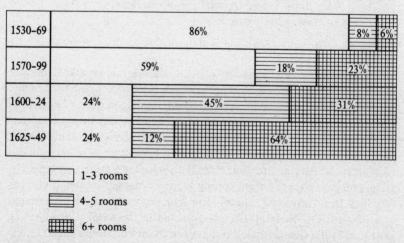

Fig. 32.   Distribution of house sizes, 1530—1649 (based on inventories)

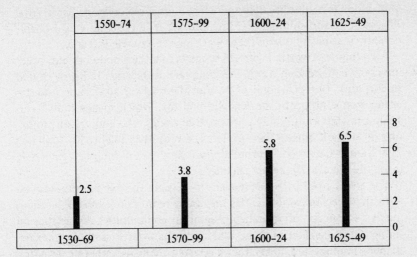

Fig. 33. Average house size — number of rooms per house, 1550—1649 (based on inventories)

size period by period, might almost be regarded as an index of building activity. The biggest spree came in the 1600—24 generation, when an average of two full rooms were added to the peasant house.

It was in this first generation of the seventeenth century, too, and the generation which followed, that the majority of peasants provided their new or extended houses with high quality, properly carpentered furniture. One only has to look at a pre-1560 inventory, with its few meagre items of household equipment and almost valueless forms, stools, trestles and table boards, to realize that early Tudor communities had little call for the products of specialized wood craftsmen. But from the first decade of the seventeenth century, in addition to the traditional carpenters and coopers, we begin to come across sawyers, turners, and even specialist joiners: just at the time when joined tables and benches, turned chairs and bedsteads are beginning to appear in local inventories. The Knowle poll tax of 1660 lists 2 sawyers, 6 carpenters, 3 coopers, 4 turners, and 2 wheelwrights.

Building crafts, other than carpentry, must also have been thriving throughout the 'Great Rebuilding' period. Bricks were in demand for ovens and chimney stacks — it was during the first generation of the seventeenth century that the latter were introduced into the majority of local peasant houses. Tiles were wanted for roofs and floors. Thomas Lynescome, one of Yardley's farmer-tilemakers (d. 1598) left 'bricke, tyle crests & gutters', fired and unfired, to the value of £4 16s. Two tilers were at work at Yardley in the first decade of the century, together with a thatcher. The first, and in fact only, bricklayer of whom we have knowledge died in 1614. But most of the chimney-building and other bricklaying was probably done by masons, of whom there were four at Knowle in 1660.

For what it is worth, Figure 28 suggests that the woodwork and building crafts expanded at much the same rate as the other industries found in the area. Out of a total of 74 craftsmen, 22 (or 30%) came into this occupational group in the Knowle poll tax, which means that it was second in importance only to the textile trades. The equivalent proportion at Solihull among the recipients of Wheatly's dole, 1650–1719 was 23%; though here wood and building workers were outnumbered not only by textile but also by metal craftsmen.

The role played by rural industry in helping the five parishes to cope with their ecological difficulties inevitably reminds one of Dr E. F. Schumacher's concept of revitalizing agrarian communities 'by adding an industrial dimension to them'. The main characteristics of his 'intermediate technology' are, firstly, that it is labour-intensive rather than capital-intensive; and, secondly, that it converts '(mainly) local materials into useful goods for (mainly) local use'.[13]

Whether or not Dr Schumacher is right in arguing that it is best for developing countries 'to go step by step up the evolutionary staircase of intermediate technologies', this analysis certainly illustrates the contention that this was a staircase 'which the developed countries themselves had to climb in history'.[14]

9

MODEL OF DEMOGRAPHIC, ECONOMIC AND SOCIAL DEVELOPMENTS, 1575–1649

In Figure 34 an attempt has been made to represent the demographic, economic and social developments under consideration in diagrammatic form. The rectangular frame is intended to signify the boundary of the five parishes. Boxes inside this frame are therefore concerned with internal developments, while those outside it represent exterior factors or inputs. A chronology has been indicated in the left-hand margin, with the key population estimates at an appropriate point on the right. As far as possible, boxes have been positioned and scaled in relation to the chronology; but, because of restrictions of layout, and also because many of the developments cannot be precisely dated, this visual chronology should be regarded as no more than approximate.

Boxes ① and ② represent what we have called the ecological equilibrium of the mid Tudor period: when a comparatively small population was gaining its livelihood — as had the previous five or six generations — by practising pasture farming, with the main emphasis on stock rearing and beef production. From the 1570s, however, this state of equilibrium is being undermined by a sharp population increase ⑤, which is due partly to internal demographic pressure ④, and partly to the fact that external demographic pressure is engendering an unprecedentedly high rate of immigration ③.

The result is, firstly, a phase of ecological disequilibrium during which there develops a serious imbalance between population size and local resources, as they were at that time being exploited: a phase which culminates in the Malthusian check of 1613—19 ⑦. This is overlapped and followed by a second phase during which, as a result of a series of negative responses ⑦, ⑧, ⑩, ⑪ [1]; and of positive responses ⑥, ⑭, ⑰, the ecological difficulties are overcome, and a new equilibrium established, with a considerably higher Malthusian ceiling.

Thus far, it seems difficult to deny the proposition that population pressure was the instigator of economic growth — i.e., agrarian and industrial development. But what this model also seems to show — and it did not in fact become apparent until the model was constructed — is that, although the demographic input clearly provided the stimulus for development, its successful pursuit was probably no less dependent on economic inputs. The spread of convertible husbandry may be regarded as one such factor ⓓ; the expanding presence of the iron industry in the Birmingham area and the Black Country ⓔ as another. But pre-eminent among the economic inputs was the price rise ⓑ.

The first and most obvious effect of the price rise, here and throughout the country, was that it greatly increased the difficulties and the sufferings of those who were landless ⑤. 'The great price rise', says Christopher Hill, 'was accompanied by a wage freeze.'[2] Between 1500 and 1640 it is estimated that the landless labourer's real wages dropped by 50%.[3] Since over the same period the prices of industrial products were increasing at a considerably slower rate than those of agricultural products, the landless craftsman could hardly have fared much better.

Nor is it difficult to exemplify the resulting hardship from local records. The postcard-sized inventory of John Rawlings, a weaver of Yardley who died in July 1614, shows that he had no land, no livestock — only apparel,

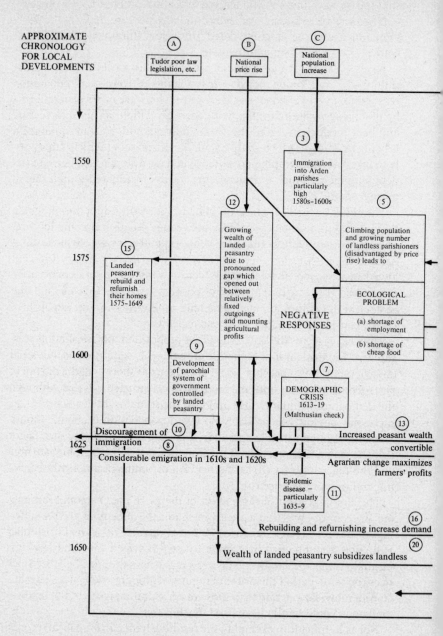

Fig. 34.   Model of demographic, economic and social developments in five north Arden parishes, 1575–1649.

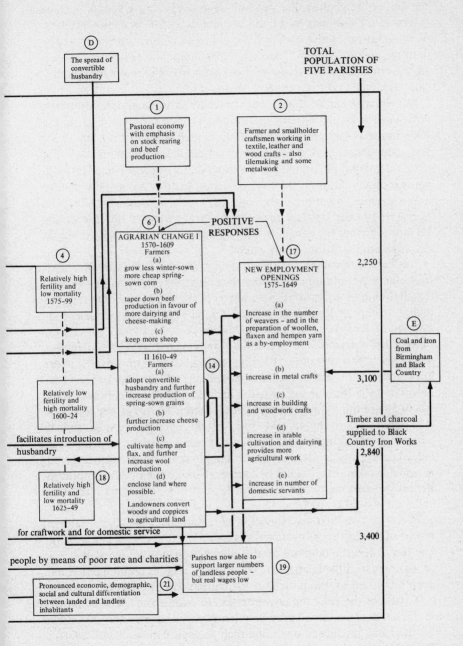

TOTAL POPULATION OF FIVE PARISHES

D · The spread of convertible husbandry

1 · Pastoral economy with emphasis on stock rearing and beef production

2 · Farmer and smallholder craftsmen working in textile, leather and wood crafts – also tilemaking and some metalwork

6 · AGRARIAN CHANGE I
1570–1609
Farmers
(a) grow less winter-sown more cheap spring-sown corn
(b) taper down beef production in favour of more dairying and cheese-making
(c) keep more sheep

II 1610–49
Farmers
(a) adopt convertible husbandry and further increase production of spring-sown grains
(b) further increase cheese production
(c) cultivate hemp and flax, and further increase wool production
(d) enclose land where possible.
Landowners convert woods and coppices to agricultural land

POSITIVE RESPONSES

17 · NEW EMPLOYMENT OPENINGS
1575–1649
(a) Increase in the number of weavers – and in the preparation of woollen, flaxen and hempen yarn as a by-employment
(b) increase in metal crafts
(c) increase in building and woodwork crafts
(d) increase in arable cultivation and dairying provides more agricultural work
(e) increase in number of domestic servants

4 · Relatively high fertility and low mortality 1575–99

Relatively low fertility and high mortality 1600–24

Relatively high fertility and low mortality 1625–49

facilitates introduction of husbandry

for craftwork and for domestic service

people by means of poor rate and charities

E · Coal and iron from Birmingham and Black Country

Timber and charcoal supplied to Black Country Iron Works

19 · Parishes now able to support larger numbers of landless people – but real wages low

21 · Pronounced economic, demographic, social and cultural differentiation between landed and landless inhabitants

2,250

3,100

2,840

3,400

14

18

bed and bedding, one coffer and two saucers. At a time when the average inventoried estate was valued at £59, his effects came to £5 4s. – of which £3 was tied up in his 'three payre of old weavers lomes & furniture their unto belonging'. In 1648 Humphrey Hodgetts, Solihull's first nailer, aged 38, 'was not able to get above 4s. a week' on which to maintain a chronically sick wife and five children, aged 1–11.[4]

But elsewhere in Solihull were many other parishioners whose lot must have been every bit as rosy as Humphrey Hodgetts's was grim. In the Arden area at least, for virtually all the landed peasantry, the late Tudor and early Stuart period is a time of unparalleled prosperity. A rising national population, bringing as it did an ever increasing demand for food, was no disadvantage to the food producer. In other parts of the country a considerable proportion of the bonanza profits may sometimes have been transferred to the landlord in the form of rent increases. But that was by no means always the case here. On the contrary, rents often lagged behind prices to a quite extraordinary extent.

Particularly fortunate in this respect were the forest's innumerable freeholders. At Solihull in 1632 the chief rents of 75 free tenants – including all the big severalty farmers – add up to £14 16s. 10d. – the value of one plough team.[5] At Knowle in 1605, 937 acres of freehold land yielded an average of 1.8d. per acre. Charles Waring, gent, held 'one Capital Messuage called Burye Hall . . . and certain lands in Longdon End' amounting to 225 acres for a rent of 8s. 11d.; plus lands called Williamsons (68½ acres) for a further 12½d. Rather higher sums were often due from customary tenants. The 1605 Knowle survey particularizes 1,127 acres of copyhold land. About 30% of this (332 acres) was rented at from 1d. to 3¾d. per acre; 47% (533 acres) at between 4d. and 7¾d.; 22% (247 acres) between 8d. and 1s. 3d.; and 1% (15 acres) at over 1s. 3d. But at a time when the sown acre was valued on average at £1 2s., even the top rate of 3s. 7½d. must have offered reasonable prospects. The Solihull survey of 1601 estimates the 'ymproved Rentes' for customary and leasehold land at £75. The actual rent being collected was £9 2s. 4d.[6]

The price rise then, had the effect of shifting the balance of wealth in favour of the farmer: as against the landless labourer or craftsman, on the one hand, and the landlord on the other ⑫. In terms of social justice – at least as far as the landless are concerned – there is nothing that could possibly be said in favour of this redistribution. Nevertheless, it is arguable that without the resulting concentration of wealth and spending power in the hands of the landed peasantry, it might well have proved impossible for the local parishes to overcome their ecological difficulties at all. For, from the economic point of view, the price rise produced what was in effect an injection of capital into this underdeveloped area: of a kind which is invariably needed today if an underdeveloped economy is to be set in motion.

We see this spontaneously injected capital at work in many different ways: so much so, that — as the model of developments shows — its effects are almost as widely diffused as those of the population increase itself. To begin with, it was probably crucial in facilitating the agrarian changes — and in particular, the introduction of convertible husbandry — which could alone satisfy the growing demand of the landless cottager for cheap corn ⑬. 'Even when the benefits of new techniques were appreciated', writes L. A. Clarkson, 'many farmers could not afford the capital outlay involved ... Convertible husbandry, for example, was ... expensive to establish and, by the early eighteenth century, it had conquered barely half the Midland lowlands and had made even less advance elsewhere.'[7] For one thing, this change-over necessitated the division of the large old pasture closes into smaller fields, by the digging of banks and ditches and the planting of hedgerows. The expense of converting the 'pasture ground called Castle Hills' into 'seaven parts' must have been considerable. More corn growing also necessitated more and bigger barns. The proportion of inventoried farmsteads with barns goes up from 32% in the period 1530—69 to 76% in the period 1610–49. Even today the fine early-seventeenth-century timber-framed barns are almost as conspicuous in the unurbanized parts of the area as are the farmsteads and cottages with which they were originally associated. Lastly, more corn meant more ploughs, harrows, draught animals, carts and wains. There were only 2 ploughs and 5 carts or wains to every 10 farms during mid Tudor times; by the early seventeenth century the corresponding figures were 8 and 19. Robert Palmer had in his 'fold yarde ... One weane body two payre of wheeles two payre of Tumbrill Draughts two Tumbrill Skirts two plowes one great harrow two little harrows and yokes and Tewes and all other tooles belonging to Husbandry' valued at £5.

Secondly, the surplus capital of the landed peasantry helped to ameliorate the other main aspect of the ecological problem, shortage of employment ⑰. Not only were more farm servants required as a result of the agrarian changes: there was more work for the blacksmith. No wheelwrights are found in the five parishes during the sixteenth century. But three are known to have followed that calling in the first half of the seventeenth; and Knowle was supporting two in 1660.

Of even greater importance is the fact that increased peasant wealth led to a rise in the demand for consumer products of every kind. The 'Great Rebuilding' and the 'Great Refurnishing' are merely the most obvious examples of this ⑮ ⑯. 'The century after 1530', it has been suggested, may have been 'that in which a significant portion of the English population was reclothed as well as rehoused'.[8] During the period 1530–69 an average of 6.4 garments are listed in specified wardrobes. In the 1570–1609 period the figure goes up to 11.4. Probably because the wardrobe was becoming too large, clothes are so infrequently detailed during the following forty-year period that it is impossible to produce an average; but the mean value of 'apparel' or 'raiment' increases from £1 4s. to £1 18s. The value of gold and silver goes up still more steeply from a mean of 16s. in the first period to £5 1s. in the third. The opening generation of the seventeenth century was the first generation ever when the son of an Arden husbandman could have been born with a silver spoon in his mouth. As far as money itself is concerned, only 1 in 8 inventories during the 1530–69 period specifies ready cash, the average amount being £1 2s. Among the 1610–49 group, 1 in 3 lists money, with an average of £2 6s. By the 1650–89 period the proportion of peasants with cash about them at death has gone up to 8 out of 10.

Apart from the contents of inventories even the way they are laid out changes significantly over this period. As a rule, early appraisers begin by listing the deceased person's cattle – for cattle mattered to them almost as much as they mattered to Abraham – only then going into the house to list the meagre domestic possessions. But during the late sixteenth and early seventeenth century this procedure becomes less and less common: and, from 1633, there is not a single inventory in which the contents of the house are not appraised first. Such a change is surely indicative of a new attitude – almost a new psychology – in which emphasis is shifting from the producer to the consumer; and domestic ease and comfort are really beginning to count for something – in more senses than one.

By the early seventeenth century the north Arden area must indeed have had 'an economy in which the demand for food, housing, furniture, fuel and so many other consumers' goods was expanding'.[9] Furthermore, this expansion of consumer demand, although it patently did not stretch to the landless cottager, does seem to have embraced every section of the landed peasantry. In housing and furnishing alike, less prosperous peasants showed improvements which were comparable with those obtained by their richer neighbours. As between the first and last forty-year periods, the value of household goods in the homes of the wealthy and substantial increased by 289% and 275% respectively; the furnishings of middling and lesser peasants by 310 and 247%.[10]

From the point of view of the peasant, all this simply meant miraculously rising living standards. But from the point of view of the local economy, it meant miraculously rising employment. Most of the 'framed' tables, 'wainscot' chairs, joined beds, stools and 'presses' were no doubt produced locally.[11] As many as 37 tailors occur over the period 1590–1719, as well as a capper and a hat-dresser. What kept the women and

children of the cottager bent over their 'breaking', 'hatchelling' and spinning but the rising demand for linen on the part of local yeomen and husbandmen. The average number of napkins goes up from 1 to 10 between
the 1530—69 and the 1610—49 periods; of table cloths from 1 to 2; of
flaxen sheets from 3 to 6.

Furthermore, furniture had to be dusted, clothes and linen washed and
ironed. The greater wealth, the bigger houses, the more cosseted life style
of the wealthy and substantial peasants meant that they wanted more
domestic service. Of the 271 females listed in the 1660 Knowle poll tax
return, 50, or 18.5% were maid-servants: many of them apparently living
in the home of their master.

Dr Peter Bowden, while acknowledging that the growing wealth of agricultural producers would have helped to stimulate industrial production,
has suggested that their 'propensity to save', and even 'to hoard', may considerably have inhibited the rate at which they were prepared to spend.[12]
In the five parishes, at least, it would appear that the peasant spent first
and saved afterwards. In Figure 35 — remembering that the farmer's rising
wealth depended on the gap which opened out between food prices and
rent — the plottings representing the local price indices of arable crops and

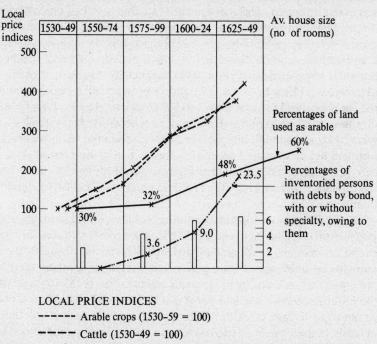

LOCAL PRICE INDICES
------ Arable crops (1530–59 = 100)
---- Cattle (1530–49 = 100)

Fig. 35.   Local price indices, 1530—1649 — and their relationship to house
size, the introduction of convertible husbandry (as indicated by proportion of
land used as arable) and the investment of risk capital

cattle may be taken as a rough indication of the growth of peasant capital. Similarly, the plottings showing the proportion of land used as arable give a rough indication of expenditure on agricultural improvement; and those showing house size a rough indication of expenditure on house improvement. From this, it would appear that local yeomen and husbandmen were quickly off the mark in spending on their farmhouse. During the first half of the seventeenth century, as well as continuing to do this, many of them must also have been using their surplus wealth to build a barn and adapt their fields to convertible husbandry.

It is as the agrarian improvements and the rebuilding approach completion that we find the local peasant beginning to think not of hoarding his money indeed — only 2 out of 135 inventories dated 1575—1649 record cash in the house over £10 — but of lending it out as risk capital. Prior to 1575 there are no instances of deceased peasants being owed monies 'with . . .' or 'without specialty', or by bond; and only one instance occurs in the last quarter of the sixteenth century. But among peasants dying 1600—24, 5 out of 56 had risk capital out on loan; and in the next generation the proportion goes up to 12 out of 51, or almost 1 in every 4. Of the 5 testators engaged in money-lending during the first quarter of the seventeenth century, one was a widow, another a retired husbandman. But the remaining 3 were apparently in mid career. George Feeld (d. 1612), a weaver-farmer of Yardley, was cultivating at least 40 acres and lived in a seven-roomed house. Nevertheless 36% of his estate, or £40, had been invested: some of it with, some without specialty. Similarly, 5 of the 12 investors who died between 1625 and 1649 were still working farmers, the sums involved ranging from 5 to 50% of their total estate. Prior to 1624 all those engaged in money-lending were of above average wealth — i.e., wealthy or substantial. But 2 of the 12 investors in the 1625—49 generation had below average estates, and 1 below half of the average. And all this risk capital, unlike hoarded savings, would presumably have been instrumental in financing still further agrarian and industrial developments.

The third main way in which surplus peasant wealth helped the local parishes to cope with their ecological difficulties depended to a considerable extent on another, so far undiscussed, but by no means negligible input: namely the influence of state policy and legislation, as these were represented and enforced by the local justices of the peace Ⓐ. In particular, the Elizabethan poor law laid down that the Overseers of the Poor of each parish were 'to raise weekly or otherwise, by taxation of every . . . occupier of lands, houses, tithes . . . such competent sum and sums of money as they shall think fit . . . towards the necessary relief of the lame, impotent, old, blind and such other among them being poor and not able to work'.[13] Here we see part of the surplus wealth of the landed peasantry, 'according to the ability of the same parish', as the 1601 act specifically states, being forcibly requisitioned in order to relieve at least the direst sufferings of the less fortunate section of the community ⓴ .

Moreover, the Crown, whose paternalistic policy over this period was in many ways quite remarkable for its ecological sensitivity, expected far more than charitable hand-outs to the impotent poor. It fully appreciated that the able-bodied poor had certain basic requirements, and made strenuous efforts to see that these were met. In the first place, such people needed to be 'adequately housed; for which purpose poor law legislation laid down that, where necessary, parish funds should be used on the building of suitable cottages. Ideally, poor households would also possess a smallholding, to give them a basis of self-sufficiency and independence. But the 4 acre act of 1589, although well enough conceived, proved too ambitious to be widely implemented. With regard to the third requirement of the poor, cheap food, the state could do little at parochial level. But, particularly in times of scarcity, it endeavoured to moderate prices by enacting that all surplus corn should be presented for sale in open market; and by taking action, through the justices, against the profiteering of engrossers and regraters. The problem of providing employment could be, and was, tackled at parochial level. The poor law act of 1601 ordered overseers to make available a convenient stock of flax, hemp, wool, thread, iron or other necessary ware and stuff to set the poor on work'.[14]

Clearly, this comprehensive state policy was very much on the lines required by the local and, no doubt, by the national ecological situation. How meticulously and how generously it was carried out is another matter. In 1634 the Yardley overseers were indicted at the Worcester Quarter Sessions 'for not providing convenient hemp flax iron and wool to set the paupers there to labour'.[15] In 1659 the Warwickshire Quarter Sessions had to compel the overseers of Bickenhill to provide a habitation for Sarah Mayou, a widow with two small children, and 'in great want'.[16]

As far as direct parochial relief is concerned, 32% of all adults buried at Solihull between 1603 and 1612 were presumably in receipt of some measure of support, for the register describes them as paupers; over the crisis period 1613—19 the corresponding figure goes up to 46%. At Bickenhill between 1630 and 1649, by contrast, the proportion of adults buried as paupers was as low as 1 in 9. In the year 1649—50, £32 16s. 6d. was levied by the Yardley overseers from approximately 116 rate-paying households, at an average of 4s. 8d. each. Two-thirds of the total was disbursed on regular pay to 13 persons, at an average rate of 2s. 7d. per month. Five widows and 2 other females received between 1s. and 4s. 8d. per month; 6 males had between 1s. 0d. and 1s. 4d. Twenty-four other parishioners were allowed occasional relief, the highest sum of 18s. going to 'William Howler and his wyfe in theire necessitie'.[17]

Solihull's run of poor law accounts covering the period 1663–80[18] shows a remarkably steady expenditure, varying from a low of £41 in 1670–1 to a high of £71 in 1674–5, but with a disbursement between £55 and £65 in ten of the sixteen years. Overall the annual mean works out at about £57, which, had it been wholly levied from the 150–160 rate-paying households, would have amounted to a charge of about 7s. 3d. per annum. In fact, roughly 20% of a typical year's total was provided by the parish bailiff out of the profits from the parochial lands. An analysis of the accounts for 1676–80 shows that over this three years there were 72 recipients, of whom 29 were men, 32 widows, 10 women other than widows, while 1 person drew payments in respect of two or more children. Slightly over 90% of the total disbursements went on regular pay which, by coincidence, averaged 2s. 7d. per month — the same amount as at Yardley thirty years before. 'Extraordinary' or occasional relief was mainly devoted to rent subsidies, house repairs, clothing and sickness payments, in roughly equal proportions. In all perhaps 1 in 4 Solihull households received a payment of some kind from the overseers; though, with only 40–45 on a monthly allowance at any one time, the proportion of regular pauper households was nearer 1 in 7.

None of this suggests dire economic distress in the mid seventeenth century, or a particularly high level of pauperization. However, there are grounds for suspecting that sometimes relief may have been administered with rather more of an eye on the rate-payers' purses than on the needs of the impoverished. In 1649, unable to make headway with the Solihull overseers, Anne Heywood has to appeal to the Warwickshire justices. Her husband had died 'about five years' previously, leaving her 'four children to maintain', which she did 'by her own labour' for three and a half years. But now, because of 'the hardness of the times', she can no longer support herself and her one remaining child. The justices order the Solihull overseers to pay her 12d. weekly.[19] Ten years later Richard Butler of Bickenhill makes a similar appeal at the Warwick Quarter Sessions. For four years he has been lame and unable to maintain himself, his wife and five children — whose ages ranged from 13 years to a few months. The inhabitants formerly allowed him 2s. 6d. per week but 'of late have refused to pay the same'. They are ordered to resume the allowance and make payment of all arrears.[20] Such cases suggest that, at any rate as far as direct parochial relief was concerned, the surplus wealth of the landed peasantry must have been pretty sparingly administered.

On the other hand — and again, this was partly due to state encouragement — there was an unusually high number of charitable bequests during this difficult period. At Solihull in 1604 Ralph and Ann Vyne and Thomas Hugford granted a yearly rent of 6s. 8d. 'for the relief of two persons in the parish'. In 1625 John Hanslappe provided £16 to 'buy land for the benefit of the poor'. Richard Averell in 1639 bequeathed 'to the poor of Solihull' a yearly rent of 3s. 4d. Edward Holbeck left £3 a year 'to the poor of Solihull' in 1645.[21] 'Mr. Thomas Wheatly's dole', instituted in 1605, to provide 10s. each annually to 'four decayed tradesmen' is yet another example of this kind of voluntary charity: which, although it was only charity, must have helped to some extent.

10

THE NEW ECOLOGICAL REGIME, 1625—74

After the culling of the 1610s, the populations of the five parishes seem again to have been growing vigorously throughout the second generation of the seventeenth century. 2,797 baptisms are recorded between 1620 and 1649, as against only 1,745 burials, giving a natural increase rate of 60%. Among couples marrying 1625—49, mean life expectation at marriage goes up by 1.4 years on the crisis generation; the childbearing span by 1.8 years (Table I and Fig. 3). Similarly, closed family size rises from 2.9 to 3.7 children; and completed family size from 4.1 to 4.4.

Meanwhile, the number of reproducing surnames, which had fallen so sharply between 1610 and 1629, is again increasing (Fig. 4). However, many of the new names — at least during the 1630s — were probably brought in by single males; for, in contrast to the previous generation (see p. 16), the surname increase is matched by a corresponding rise in the number of marriages (Fig. 5). Eight people are known to have erected cottages on the Solihull commons between 1632 and 1647; but most of them seem to have been of native stock rather than recent immigrants.[1]

There were high mortalities in the years 1635—9. Yet although a scarcity of corn is reported for Warwickshire in 1638 and 1639,[2] there are no signs of dearth locally. Burials rise in the registers, but baptisms remain well above them (Fig. 20). Almost certainly, the main cause of the trouble was epidemic disease. Nationally, the five years 1646—51 brought a run of bad harvests, and the Warwick Quarter Sessions records speak of 'the

present dearth' in 1647 and 'this hard and miserable time' in 1649.[3] Local families undoubtedly suffered: it was in the latter year that Anne Heywood went to the justices because of 'the hardness of the times', while in 1648 Humphrey Hodgetts, the Solihull nailer, had complained to them, amongst other things, of 'the poorness of his trade'.[4] But again, the registers — although defective — do not suggest serious demographic trouble (Fig. 36).

On the other hand, by the third quarter of the seventeenth century it is possible that population pressure was again tending to build up to a point where Malthusian constraints began to threaten. The national dearth of 1657—61 could well have affected north Arden parishes (Fig. 36). Burials were not particularly high; but conceptions certainly appear to have faltered during 1657 and 1658, when Professor Hoskins categorizes the harvests as being 'deficient' and 'bad' respectively.[5] 1659, 1660 and 1661, classed as 'deficient', 'deficient' and 'dearth', however, were apparently relatively innocuous locally. In any case, even in the earlier years the only parish to show a substantial shortfall in conceptions was Solihull where the standard of registration, though better than in the late forties and early fifties, remained suspect. There are 11 blank months in the baptism register over the five years 1657—61, as against an average of only 6 per decade in the better recorded first forty years of the century. Only 3 baptisms are to be found between 26 August 1658 and 6 February 1659; and only 1 between 25 November 1659 and 4 March of the following year. It is likely, therefore,

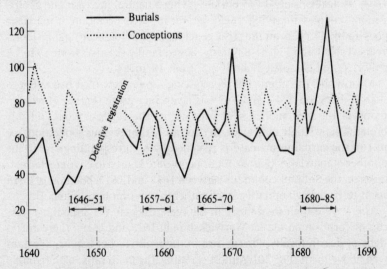

Fig. 36.   Burials and live conceptions by harvest year, 1640—89 — Sheldon, Solihull and Yardley

that to a considerable extent at least the shortfall was in the recording of baptisms, rather than in the baptisms themselves.

The registers suggest a further period of natural decrease over the years 1665—70. Despite the fact that these were 'good' and 'abundant' years according to Professor Hoskins, we now find a significant excess of burials over conceptions, not only at Solihull, but also at Yardley and Sheldon. But the deficiency in conceptions is spread fairly evenly over the harvest year. And contrary to what one would expect in the case of serious food shortage, burials tend to be unusually low in the last quarter. The particularly high mortalities of 1670 were almost certainly due to epidemic disease. At Solihull 30 burials occur between August and January, as against only 16 thereafter, while at Yardley and Sheldon there are 19 and 11 respectively between August and October. Similar late summer/early autumn burial peaks are found at Solihull in 1666, 1667 and 1669; and in 1668 and 1669 at Sheldon and Yardley. Additional evidence against food shortage is provided by the Solihull poor law accounts which are relatively low over the period 1665—70, averaging a disbursement of £52 as against a general mean for the 16 years 1663—80 of £57. Indeed in the two highest mortality years 1669 and 1670 they amount to only £44 and £41 respectively.

But perhaps the best indication that the difficulties of the fifties and sixties were not of the same order as those experienced in the 1610s, even if to some extent they were of the same kind, is the fact that the demographic rates of the cohort marrying between 1650 and 1674 remained almost as favourable as those of its immediate predecessor (Table I, Fig. 3), with a mean childbearing span of 11.1 years and closed and completed family sizes of 3.5 and 4.4 respectively.

Nor, despite the decline in the number of events recorded in the registers, is there any reason to suppose that population totals fell in the third quarter of the seventeenth century. The last satisfactory Cox estimate it is possible to obtain is that for the 1630s which works out at about 3,400. The hearth tax returns of the 1660s and 1670s imply a similar figure (Table X, p. 116).

In fact it seems unlikely that the population moved very much either above or below 3,400 during the rest of the century. For what it is worth, the registers yield an overall natural increase of 27% between 1650 and 1674. But the surplus people presumably moved elsewhere, as indeed a considerable number must have done during the previous quarter century when, despite a 60% natural increase, the actual population growth was only about 20%.

So somewhere in the region of 3,400 may well have represented the new high water mark, as it were: a figure which, as the difficulties of the 1650s and 1660s perhaps indicate, could not in any circumstances be much exceeded. Nevertheless, even this figure implies a population density of about 1 household to 37 acres: which was well in advance of anything that had been achieved — or could have been achieved — under the old ecological regime.

However, if the five parishes had made unprecedented economic progress and, in so doing, lifted the local Malthusian ceiling by as much as 50%, this had unfortunately been achieved at a considerable social cost.

11

THE SOCIAL COST

Some indication of the social structure which had developed in north Arden by the mid seventeenth century may be gained from the hearth tax returns. A combined analysis of those for Bickenhill (1663), Sheldon (1674), Solihull (1663) and Longdon (1662)[1] shows that 31 out of a total of 475 householders, or 6.5%, were charged on 4 + hearths (Fig. 37). This batch of wealthy inhabitants included a knight, and also 10 of the 13 'gentlemen' named in the lists. Eighty-five substantial or middling peasants, representing 17.9% of householders, paid on 2 or 3 hearths; 170, or 35.8%, were lesser husbandmen, smallholders, small craftsmen and labourers paying on only one. The largest category, however, consisted of people who were exempt from the tax on grounds of poverty: the vast majority of them, doubtless, being landless cottagers. They numbered 189 and represented 39.8% of households.

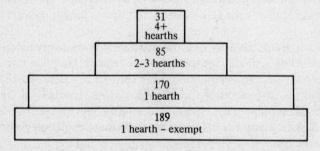

Fig. 37.   The 'social pyramid' as indicated by the hearth tax returns — Bickenhill, Sheldon, Solihull and Longdon

Of the estimated population total of the five parishes in the mid seven-teenth century (i.e., 3,400), 40% would amount to 1,360. Even allowing for the fact that some exempt households must have consisted of widows or elderly married couples living on their own, and would therefore have been of below average size, it seems likely that those belonging to landless families would have numbered 1,000 to 1,100.[2] Or, in other words, they would have been almost equivalent numerically to the whole population increase since the 1570s —i.e., an estimated 1,200. A hundred years before, in the mid sixteenth century, it is doubtful whether there would have been more than a hundred such people in the five parishes.

It is inevitable that a structural transformation of this magnitude should bring to mind that well-attested concept of sixteenth- and seventeenth-century historians, 'the polarization of society'. Yet to the long-established peasantry of the area, the alarming growth in the number of poor families must have looked less like a polarization of the old traditional society than the arising in their midst of a wholly new society.

And indeed, the polarization process in these north Arden communities does seem rather different from that described by Margaret Spufford, for instance, in her study of Chippenham, Cambridgeshire. There, as a result of a deliberate manorial policy of converting copyhold tenures to lease-hold, and the engrossment and selling out which accompanied it, 'the small farmers had been forced out at some point between 1560 and 1636'; so that by 1720 'three-quarters of the inhabitants had a house and a couple of acres at most'.[3] At Chippenham, in other words, the middle was re-moved from the local community: a community, incidentally, which saw no real change of size between the mid sixteenth and the mid seventeenth centuries.

As Dr Spufford herself points out, the type of polarization found at Chippenham would seem to resemble 'the sort of activity which Tawney thought was one of the main causes of the agrarian problem of the six-teenth century'.[4] The type of polarization found in our parishes clearly does not. For the distinctive characteristic of the process here is not a bifurcation within the old traditional local communities themselves, but rather their numerical extension. No one was displaced; on the contrary, perhaps as many as two hundred additional households were established in the five parishes between the 1570s and the 1640s. But unfortunately, although, as a result of the series of adjustments already described, these extra house-holds could be supported, it was very much a case of only just. And it was this ecological tightness which produced a degree of impoverishment that, to the landless themselves, must have seemed every bit as unendur-able as that occasioned elsewhere by engrossment and eviction.

The human suffering involved is not in question. Yet, however uniform in result, it seems important that the contrasting origin of these two types of polarization should be distinguished. The Chippenham type might perhaps be called 'direct'; that exemplified in Arden 'indirect' or 'contingent'. One of the most readily identifiable characteristics of the former is that it is not causally linked to population growth; indirect polarization, by contrast, is so linked — indeed, it is by definition contingent upon it.

It is also arguable that with the latter type of polarization conscious and deliberate exploitation need not have been involved. Rather, the inequity — and there was still plenty of that — was built into the system. Above all, it was the high food prices, which were in turn due to a rapidly rising national population, that tended to create at one and the same time affluence for those with land, and penury for those without.

Dealing with the growth of a landless class in England between 1500 and 1750, Sir J. H. Clapham wrote a quarter of a century ago that 'though we often come across consolidations and evictions . . . it is safest to connect the growth of this class mainly with the probable doubling of total population which these two and a half centuries witnessed.'[5] The Arden evidence would tend to support this insight as being at least as relevant to the phenomenon of polarization as a whole, as the currently more prevalent Tawneyite interpretation.

The polarization line within the local communities of north Arden was between householders who financed and administered the poor rate, and those who merely received it. No poor levies survive but a study of people serving parochial offices at Solihull over the period 1642—64 shows that of the 115 officers who can be traced in the hearth tax returns between 1663 and 1674, as many as 61, or 53%, paid on only one hearth. Landless craftsmen and labourers are not to be found, although some of them undoubtedly paid the poor rate. On the other hand, smallholders with 4 or 5 acres quite often took their turn at the chore of serving as one of the seven surveyors of the highways who had to be elected annually. At Chippenham polarization had pushed the inhabitant with a few acres down in the social scale. Here it almost had the effect of lifting him up. With 4 out of 10 parishioners beneath him in the socio-economic scale, even the smallholder could feel himself to be a member of the parochial establishment: from one point of view at least, among 'the best sorte of the parishe'.

It is easy in this context to understand Gregory King's stark view of English society at the end of the seventeenth century, and to appreciate its derivation. Those whom he describes as 'increasing the wealth of the kingdom' were synonymous at parochial level with the ratepayers and parish officers — basically the old, traditional community — and those 'decreasing the wealth of the kingdom' with the 'nouveau' poor, the landless, who were an actual or potential charge on the parish.[6]

From time to time the vagaries of human existence naturally resulted in rate-paying inhabitants or their widows finding themselves in need of parochial relief. Yet, at Solihull anyway, this Gregory King-like distinction was preserved even in these circumstances. In the poor law accounts of the 1660s, with the exception of widows, the names of the bulk of recipients are recorded without titles. Among the generality of entries, however, from time to time one comes across a person described as 'Goodman' or 'Goodwyfe'. These were ratepayers who had fallen on bad times.

Undoubtedly the most convenient place to observe the full complexity of the social structure in a pre-industrial English village was in the parish church, when the local community composed itself into its carefully ordered Sunday tableau — overtly at least — for the hearing of divine service. At Solihull a spate of pew building had begun in the 1580s and continued throughout the early decades of the seventeenth century. This was yet another expression of peasant affluence, running parallel with and echoing the 'Great Rebuilding' itself. Since inhabitants were at first allowed to erect their own seats, the result became so 'ununiform and irregular' that in 1679 the parish authorities felt compelled to initiate a 'decent and convenient' re-seating.[7] After its completion the top 29 families took up their places under the central tower and at the east end of the nave, grouped about the pew of Andrew Archer, Esq., 'Lord of the said Manor but now at sea' and of Henry Greswold, 'Minister of the Parish of Solihull'. The Palmers, the Botts, the Dyalls and the Tandys had erected these pews at their own 'cost and charges', with the result that they were 'appropriated in perpetuity' to the 'Mansion House' in which each resided.

Further back, in the central part of the nave and aisles, the lesser yeomen and husbandmen occupied pews which had been built 'at the Common Charge' for renting out. A comparison of mid-seventeenth-century pew rents with the hearth tax returns shows that many 1 hearth families could afford to take on such pews. Smallholders, on the other hand, are never found paying pew rent; so they must have occupied common benches behind the pews of the husbandmen. All the same, even they were no doubt distinctly separated off in their turn from the landless labourers and the 'decayed tradesmen', whose appointed place was on the poor benches beyond the south door and the poor box, well away from all their betters.

Out in the week-day world, the gentlemen and substantial yeomen who occupied the 29 top pews and 'Mansion Houses' would have enjoyed a life style which was as far removed from the small husbandman's as his was in turn from that of the landless cottager. While the husbandman toiled on his own land, the farm of the gentleman — and to a considerable extent, that of the substantial yeoman too — would have been cultivated by hired labour. Even in the mid seventeenth century most husbandmen were still using their hall for food preparation and cooking; and their ground-floor parlour as the best bedroom. The parlour of the gentleman, by contrast, had long since been converted into a comfortably furnished sitting room, while at the lower end of the house he generally had, not merely a kitchen with a well-equipped cooking hearth, but a full range of other service rooms. Many luxuries had infiltrated into the home of the lesser peasantry over the late Tudor and early Stuart period: joined furniture, flaxen sheets, even napkins and pewter tableware. But to find window curtains, a warming pan, a chamber pot — or, still more, a close stool — one would have to visit the homes of wealthy or substantial parishioners.

Historically, many of the most prestigious freeholders owed their superior position, first and foremost, to the economic depression of the late fourteenth and fifteenth centuries, when contracting population and failing peasant families had enabled their predecessors to build up holdings of 80 acres or more. In a sense, therefore, the social structure which had developed in north Arden by the mid seventeenth century was the product of two entirely separate polarizations. Starting from the early Middle Ages, when the spread of peasant wealth appears to have been relatively flat, the first — which was associated with a period of population decline — stretched the local community upwards, as it were, in terms of wealth and status, and provided it with a 'peasant aristocracy'. The second which was associated with the period of population expansion that followed stretched it downwards and provided a 'rural proletariate'. As has been shown, the big families, having established their supremacy during the late medieval contraction, benefited still further from the economic developments of the late sixteenth and early seventeenth century. In absolute terms, though not necessarily proportionately, they also benefited a great deal more than the lesser freemen and copyholders. As a result, by Stuart times gentlemen and substantial yeomen had come to dominate local society more strongly than ever before: not only economically, but socially and culturally. While farming out the more onerous parochial duties across the full body of the landed peasantry, a relatively small group of leading families tended to keep the key offices in their own hands. Thus, whereas over the period 1642–64 only 7 out of every 20 Solihull surveyors of the highways lived in houses with 2 + hearths, 13 out of 20 churchwardens did so, and 17 out of 20 parish bailiffs. At both Yardley and Solihull the feoffees of the charity estates consisted exclusively of wealthy and substantial inhabitants.

It was on the initiative of these increasingly influential bodies that a village school was founded at Solihull during the Elizabethan period and an old one revived at Yardley.[8] The endowments of Solihull's chantry chapels were first used to provide the salary of a schoolmaster in the 1560s.

By 1612 so many parishioners were availing themselves of educational facilities that the feoffees appointed an usher to assist the schoolmaster. Three years later £31 was made available by the Collector of the Parish Rents 'towards the building of the Schole', of which £5 3s. 8d. consisted of the 'free gifts of the gentry and the rest of the parishioners'.[9] The schoolmaster was required to instruct his pupils in 'the Church Catechism & in good manners, & to read write & understand English, Latine & Greek, & to cast Accompt the best he can', 'and that so farr as to fitt them for the University'.[10]

As is generally the case, it is difficult to assess the effect of these provisions. We certainly know that the sons of local gentlemen and wealthy yeomen were going up to university from the early seventeenth century. John Dolphin, the son of Edmund Dolphin of Yardley, was a student at Pembroke College, Oxford in 1624, being then aged 16.[11] Richard Pretty, son of Thomas Pretty of Yardley — and from 1636 to 1683 Rector of Aldridge, Staffordshire — must have been up at Oxford at about the same time.[12] Between 1642 and 1664, 49 parishioners were required to sign their name in the Solihull Church Book. Forty-two did so, a mere 7 making their mark. Moreover, on other occasions — somewhat enigmatically — all but one of the latter managed to sign the parish register as churchwardens. However, no absolute conclusions may be drawn from this analysis. It refers only to parish officers who were invited to sign; and there may well have been a tendency to restrict this invitation to those who were able to do so. In any case the 'casting' was not all that good in the mid-seventeenth-century parish accounts, for they are invariably 'allowd (save all miscastings)' — and checking confirms that this was not without reason.

Bibles and occasionally other books start to appear in inventories — other than those of parsons — in the first generation of the seventeenth century. By the 1625—49 period 1 in every 12 inventoried households contained reading material of some kind. For the most part, it would seem that books, like warming pans and chamber pots, tended to be a luxury confined to households of above average wealth. But there was one interesting exception. No doubt Margaret Spufford is substantially right when she argues that 'the children of labourers and farmers of holdings of only average size would have had little prospect of acquiring even a rudimentary education in the sixteenth and seventeenth centuries, even if provision existed for it'.[13] Nevertheless the inventory of William Bane, labourer of Yardley, suggests that the requirement placed on the Solihull schoolmaster — and presumably his Yardley counterpart — to 'teach & instruct all the sons of any the Inhabitants'[14] was not exclusively a pious hope. Bane, who died in 1614 leaving an estate of just under £9, must have been a bachelor or widower, for he was lodging in somebody else's house, probably that of his master. Despite this, he had 'two small coffers' of his own, and slept on his own 'Course Chaffe bedd', with 'the Course furniture to the same belonginge'. 'Money found in his coffer' came to 14s; and there was also 'money in the keeping of John Marston . . . £6', and 'in the keeping of Richard Brown . . . 8s. 2d.'. Finally, in his room, alongside the tools of his calling — 'one hoke', 'one old litell Bill' and 'other od Implements' — the appraisers came across 'Sertayne small bookes', which they valued at 10s., and 'one penne and inke horne'.

William Bane's unexpected inventory provides a timely reminder that just as the landed peasantry on the one hand were by no means a homogeneous class, neither were the landless inhabitants on the other. The wretched destitution experienced by people like John Rawlings and Humphrey Hodgetts must have been all too common. Yet poor craftsmen, like Symon Rotton, the Yardley cutler, seem to have just about managed to eke a living. Although without land or cattle, Rotton lived in a four-roomed house. And if he had to sleep on a 'chaffe-bedde', this was at least made a bit more comfortable by the addition of a 'feather boulster' and 'feather pyllowe'. One landless labourer, William Cotterell of Bickenhill (d. 1640), was even able to indulge in a little money-lending. Out of a total estate of £15 10s., he had £2 invested 'by specialty' and £5 'without specialty'. However, like William Bane, Cotterell clearly had no house to maintain, and could well have been a bachelor. It is quite possible, too, that the £7 out on loan — which is suggestively close to Bane's financial assets — represented a lifetime's savings.

The contrasts between landless cottagers and smallholders — i.e., those below and immediately above the polarization line — are difficult to demonstrate statistically: mainly because so few of the landless left a will or had their goods and chattels inventoried. We know from the 1605 Knowle survey that at the beginning of a generation when the average house size among the inventoried peasantry rose to 5.8 rooms, 20 out of 34 landless cottagers in that manor lived in a house of a half to one and a half bays. And there can be little doubt that these dwellings would have been single storied. Six smallholders with between 4 and 5¼ acres, on the other hand, had an average house size of 2.5 bays.

Rents tended to be highest amongst those with the smallest holdings. Thus at Knowle in 1605, 16 with between 2 and 5¼ acres of land paid at an average annual rent of 3d. per rood. The equivalent figure for 19 with 1 rood or less was 8d. Presumably this discrepancy was partly due to the fact that the larger cottage holdings had tended to be established fairly early during the sixteenth-century population build-up, when land was still relatively plentiful, and therefore cheap. But by the turn of the century scarcity was no doubt leading — as far as new settlers were concerned —

to greatly inflated rent charges. John Holton had to pay William Wheigham 1s. 8d, per annum for his cottage of 3 bays and 1 rood of land. Henry Bowater owed John Saunders 6s. 6d. for his 2 bay messuage and 1½ acres. And this in the same survey that lists Charles Waring as holding a capital messuage and 225 acres for 8s. 11d.

Statistics calculated for reconstituted families of different hearth tax categories (Table VI) tend to confirm, what has been suggested earlier, that socio-economic status had a profound influence on demographic performance. In these admittedly small samples men from exempt households married almost 4 years younger than their substantial and wealthy contemporaries paying on 2 + hearths: that is to say, at a mean of 25.3 years as against 29.1. However, whereas exempt males married women who averaged 2 years older than themselves, the wives of the substantial and wealthy were over 4 years younger than their husbands. The fact that exempt women entered wedlock at a mean age of 27.3 years, while substantial and wealthy females did so at 24.7, must have been one reason the poor tended to have smaller families. Their shorter life expectation at marriage — 52.4 as against 55.3 — indicating as it does, a higher proportion of foreshortened unions, would have been another. At 3.4 children, the closed family size of exempt couples marrying 1650—74 was considerably higher than the 2.1 calculated for their approximate equivalents in the 1600—24 crisis cohort (Table IV, p. 28). However, it was still well short of the mean for householders with 2 + hearths which works out at 4.5 children. As one would expect, too, the landless tended to have

TABLE VI *Demographic rates of hearth tax categories — persons marrying at Solihull and Yardley, 1650—74 (figure in brackets gives size of sample)*

	Exempt	1 hearth	2 + hearths
Mean age of males at first marriage	25.3 (10)	29.9 (18)	29.1 (21)
Mean age of females at first marriage	27.3 (8)	29.8 (10)	24.7 (14)
Mean length of union	19.6 (8)	20.1 (26)	22.0 (27)
Mean life expectation at marriage (male and female)	52.4 (14)	60.4 (27)	55.3 (29)
Closed family size	3.4 (12)	3.0 (27)	4.5 (29)
Infant mortality (number of infant deaths per 1,000 births)	147 (34)	77 (39)	56 (54)

greater difficulty in rearing their offspring. Whereas the infant mortality rate among families with 2 + hearths works out at a mere 56 per 1,000, that for the exempt was 147 per 1,000. Table VI also suggests that in general farmers and smallholders paying on only 1 hearth came between the two extremes already discussed — though in this analysis they turn out to have a higher life expectation than married couples with 2 + hearths, and a lower closed family size than the exempt.

Case histories of three families towards the bottom end of the socio-economic scale provide interesting contrasts, and demonstrate how blurred the line could sometimes be between those who — to revert to Gregory King's terminology — 'increased the wealth' of the parish and those who 'decreased' it. The Metcalfs, although they moved into Solihull as an already married couple in the late 1590s, had been lucky enough to acquire a 4 acre holding at Tilehouse Green, which, since it is described in the Knowle survey of 1605 as 'lately Julian Harbornes and before that John Brandons', had clearly been in existence for some time. Indeed, it may well have originated as one of the 4 acre intakes made from the waste in accordance with Elizabethan statute. The 1605 survey describes Richard Metcalf's land as 'one orchard and three crofts', while his cottage was of $2\frac{1}{2}$ bays, so that there were probably only two or three rooms. In this house Joan Metcalf gave birth to five children over a period of 9 years 3 months. Two died in infancy, however, and two others — a boy and a girl — presumably left the parish to settle elsewhere. John, the oldest surviving child, probably took over the Tilehouse Green smallhold-ing on, or just before, his father's death in August 1631. Certainly his first recorded child was baptized at Solihull in January 1631: it seeming likely that a little prior to this — and therefore at the age of about 30 — he had married his wife Frances in a nearby parish. In any event, during the next 9 years four other children were born to this couple; and, unlike the previous generation, they all appear to have been reared successfully. Again, however, only the eldest boy, John II, remained in the parish; and he did not marry — or presumably take over the family holding — until 1666, when he was 33 years of age. We do not know what Richard Metcalf, or the two Johns who succeeded him, did for a living. But with their 4 acre holding, they were certainly able to maintain their indepen-dence. None of them ended up as paupers; and although omitted from the hearth tax returns, they would doubtless have been chargeable on one hearth. Indeed, John I even served in the least regarded of parish offices, being nominated as surveyor of the highways for his own quarter of the parish in 1635 and 1636, while John II acted in the same capacity in 1674.

The Rastells, a long-established Solihull family, held only 'one dwelling house and the backside', amounting to 1 rood of land.[15] Thomas and Anne Rastell, who married in 1584, aged 30 and 17 respectively, had a family of four boys. But although they all seem to have been reared successfully, the second and third died at Solihull in middle life, apparently unmarried, while the youngest son must have moved elsewhere. As with the Metcalfs, the eldest inherited the family tenement, though by the time John married in 1618, almost four years after his father's death, he himself was 33 and his bride 37. Not surprisingly, John had only two children; as indeed, did the next John, who had to wait until he was 46 before acquiring the cottage and marrying, on the death of his mother in 1663. Despite their lowly estate, the Rastells paid on 1 hearth in 1662 and 1670; though by 1671, John II having died in the previous year, the Widow Rastell was exempt. In the main, however, the Rastells must have managed to pay their poor rate. For when John II is sick in 1667–8, it is Goodwife Rastell who receives a 2s. 6d. necessity payment on his behalf.

A good example of a family who decreased the wealth of the parish were the Brockhursts. It was in 1657, at the comparatively early age of 19, that John Brockhurst married Catherine Ward at Solihull. Nothing is known of their holding, but over 12 or 13 years Catherine gave birth to five children. The firstborn died a couple of months before his third birthday, but no other child burials are recorded. The family, however, must have been extremely poor. Even in 1663 when John, who was a tailor by trade, had only one child to support, he was already exempt from the hearth tax. By 1669 the Brockhursts had three youngsters, aged 8, 5 and 2. It was in this year that John was nominated to receive Wheatly's dole. Since his earnings are unlikely to have been more than four or five shillings a week, the resulting 10s 0d. would have represented a considerable subsidy. However, it was not enough. A further child was on the way, and this led the Brockhursts to apply for poor relief. In 1669/70 the Shirley overseer gave John 3s. 0d. for 'a strike of corn . . . upon his wife's lying in'. During the poor law year 1670–1 he received a further 'extraordinary' payment of 5s. 6d. 'in his want'. The following year Catherine's health broke down, the overseer paying John Brockhurst's wife 4s. 10d. 'when she was lame and sicke'. Worse was to come. Though his burial is not recorded, John himself presumably died in late 1672 or early 1673, at the age of about 36. Without a breadwinner, it was now of course impossible for the family to manage on its own. So during 1673–4 Widow Brockhurst received 6 regular monthly payments of 4s. 6d., followed by a further 6 at 5s. 0d. She remained on the parish books throughout the poor law year 1674–5, still drawing 5s. 0d. per month. But in May of the following year the payments were cut back to 4s. 0d.; and five months later they were discontinued altogether. By this time Catherine's children were aged 15, 13, 9 and 6. The two eldest would certainly have been capable of working; and the family's most difficult period from the financial point of view was over. There is a gap in the Solihull poor law accounts from 1680–1 to 1689–90. When they are resumed in 1690–1[16] we find that Catherine Brockhurst, widow, is again in receipt of regular monthly payments, this time of 2s. 0d. per month. But now the relief is being allowed because of her 'dimsighted-ness, sicklyness, lameness and age'.

There was naturally a tendency for landless cottagers to congregate on surviving greens and commons. In 1660, according to the Knowle poll tax, Widney End, which had an extensive area of waste known as Copt Heath, harboured no less than 11 small craftsmen and 9 labourers, out of a total of 26 taxable adult males. In Longdon End, on the other hand, where little common waste was available, 9 out of 39 adult males followed a craft and 5 were labourers. Rather surprisingly, the 1663 hearth tax records a mere 21% of Widney householders as exempt from payment on grounds of poverty, which is well below the parochial average, and about the same as at Longdon. The three other Solihull ends which had substantial stretches of waste, however, show an above average proportion of exempt households: Shirley with 54%, Forshaw with 50% and Whitlocks with 43%.

Although a presentment of the Minister and Churchwardens of Yardley reported that there were no 'conventicles or other meetings' in 1674, the neighbouring parish of King's Norton had a Quaker meeting: which the two Yardley Quakers named on the same occasion presumably attended. Indeed, King's Norton had been one of the four places in Worcestershire to possess a Puritan lectureship prior to the Civil War.[17] A Presbyterian meeting was being 'held in the barn of Anne Webb, widow, at Knowle' in 1689; while a year later Quarter Sessions licensed a Quaker meeting at 'the dwelling house of Frances Palmers on Fulford heath'.[18] The location of Anne Webb's barn is unknown, but since Ful-ford Heath was in the extreme south of Solihull, about 5 miles from the parish church, this meeting at least would seem to fit in with Professor Alan Everitt's idea that remote squatter communities were particularly prone to foster dissent.[19]

A comparison of the Compton census of 1676 with an index of local recusants suggests that the former's tally of 49 Nonconformists for the five parishes, which represents 3.1% of the total communicants, was probably an underestimate. Nevertheless, nonconformity was far from rampant in north Arden: and that, despite its particularly strong showing along the eastern flank of the Birmingham Plateau — especially in the Bedworth, Coventry and Kenilworth areas — and in Birmingham itself, only a few miles to the west. In general Catholicism may have been even weaker. But at Solihull the Compton census and the local recusancy index suggest a figure of about 10%. The economic and social developments reviewed in the present study may have been partly responsible. For the hearth tax returns reveal that a nucleus of Catholics belonged to the class of prominent freeholders who had benefited so much from the price rise. The Warings, who had 10 hearths, were staunch Catholics; so were the Hugfords with 8, and the Neweys with 5. Arguably, the presence of these wealthy and prestigious families was one of the factors that helped to keep the old faith so much stronger at Solihull than elsewhere: its enormous parochial area and the remoteness of many of its farmsteads and hamlets being others.

As one would expect, Catholic — and also Nonconformist — recusants generally refrained from hiring a pew in the parish church, and their names only very rarely occur in the parish register. But they were by no means ostracized from the local community. Between 1612 and 1679 an estimated 59 Papists and Nonconformists served parish offices on approximately 112 occasions — i.e., at an average of roughly twice each. Bearing in mind that women did not normally serve in any case, this means that something like 1 in 4 recusants took an active part in parochial administration: a proportion which is not likely to have differed greatly from that found among the rest of the community. The commonest post, as always, was that of surveyor of the highways. But all the other offices were obviously open to recusants, if indeed they were not required to serve them under some form of house-row system.

Of the 57 Catholics and Nonconformists — the records frequently fail to distinguish between the two — who can be tentatively traced in the hearth tax returns, between 25 and 30 — depending on the exclusion or inclusion of doubtful name identifications — were exempt. If one takes the lower figure, this means that 44% of recusants were adjudged too poor to pay the tax. The higher figure, on the other hand, would yield a proportion of 53%. That recusancy was strong among the poorer sections of the community is further confirmed by the fact that about 45 out of an estimated total of 258 Solihull male recusants can be identified among the recipients of Wheatly's dole for 'decayed tradesmen'.

PART THREE

IMPLICATIONS

12

GENERAL PROPOSITIONS

From the demographic trough of the late fourteenth century, England's pre-industrial population growth seems to have taken place in two distinct phases. The first began in the late fifteenth century and culminated three generations later in the vicious, though relatively short, demographic cut-back of the 1550s. The second coincided with the 25 year-long run of unusually favourable harvests which spanned the years 1566–93 (broken only in 1573 and 1587). But then, what Professor Hoskins has called 'the Great Famine' of the mid 1590s ushered in a period of the most profound demographic disturbance, which persisted for a full half century.

Some historians have interpreted this long, painful climacteric as a major Malthusian check caused by the cumulative pressure of the previous century's population growth on inadequate resources. However, as it stands, this interpretation raises certain difficulties. Firstly, in a straightforward Malthusian situation one would expect population growth to be halted and, indeed, the total to fall. But in fact neither of these things happened over the half century in question. On the contrary, although each decade from the 1590s to the 1640s brought years of serious food shortage and devastating epidemics, the national population total continued to grow steadily: perhaps increasing by a million between the 1590s and the 1630s — or in other words, by as much as 20%.

A second puzzling feature of this particular period of demographic difficulty is that it was also one of unprecedented economic advance. For these were the very years when the 'agricultural revolution' of Dr Kerridge and the 'industrial revolution' associated with Professor Nef were coming to fruition.

It was this paradox that led the late J. D. Chambers in his final book to argue that, whereas the demographic crisis of the early fourteenth century 'shows every condition of a Malthusian crisis', 'the assumption of a Malthusian check in the late sixteenth and early seventeenth centuries remains unproven'.[1]

The explanation of these apparent inconsistencies would seem to lie in the fact that, unlike the fourteenth-century demographic crisis, that of

the seventeenth century was met by an at least partially successful reaction: a reaction which manifested itself in the form of agrarian and
industrial development and which, despite the persistent ravages of famine and disease, enabled the country for the first time ever to carry its population beyond the 5 million mark. England was not, indeed, the passive
victim of a Malthusian check — to that extent Chambers was right. But it
was wrestling desperately during these years with a Malthusian predicament of alarming proportions — or in other words, with serious and prolonged ecological difficulties.[2]

If these assertions have any validity, then the course of events in the
parishes of north Arden during Elizabethan and early Stuart times would
seem to reflect what was happening in the country at large. In north
Arden, as in England generally, a long period of sustained and exuberant
population growth culminated in a critical demographic malaise. But
because the population growth and the malaise were accompanied by
economic development — to a degree, the 'revolutions' of Kerridge and
Nef are both traceable in the five parishes — the local communities were
eventually able to overcome their difficulties. The 'Malthusian check' did
not check. Despite it — even, perhaps, because of it — local population continued to advance: only levelling off — as indeed did the national population itself — when the plateau level which was to be sustained throughout
the second half of the seventeenth century had been reached.

It is not of course suggested that the chronology of the Arden climacteric, still less the precise mechanism of its reaction, is capable of being
extended beyond the bounds of the five parishes themselves. Nevertheless,
the following propositions which have been derived from, or suggested by,
this study may be worth testing more widely.

*I That population growth in the late sixteenth and early seventeenth centuries
brought a state of ecological disequilibrium to many English rural communities —
i.e., a serious imbalance between population and resources — and that in some
cases this led to a distinct Malthusian check.*

In south Warwickshire, western Northamptonshire, Leicestershire and
Oxfordshire ecological difficulties are likely to have been particularly
marked in the first decade of the seventeenth century, reaching a peak
in the years 1606–9, when they may have been a factor in precipitating
the Midland Revolt.[3]

For the central midlands, based on the Birmingham Plateau, it looks
as if the 1610s were more crisis prone. A recent study of Staffordshire
registers suggests 'that dearth was abroad in the second and third decades
of the century'; while a graph for ten parishes in the Birmingham area

(including Solihull and Yardley) shows the same slump in baptisms and rise in burials which are recorded on the comparable graph for the five parishes in the 1610s (Fig. 5).[4] This decade may also have been a critical one in parts of eastern England, where Dr Spufford finds that two of the three Cambridgeshire communities she has examined in detail had 'years of crisis' during the period 1612–18.[5]

In the north of England the ecologically most disastrous decade was undoubtedly the 1620s, with spasms of exceptionally high mortality in Cumberland, Westmorland, parts of Lancashire, and in the West Riding of Yorkshire: including established 'crises of subsistence' at Greystock and Ashton-under-Lyne in the harvest year 1623–4.[6]

II That the reaction of local communities to ecological difficulties varied widely from place to place. But that, nevertheless, if a sufficient number of detailed studies of the phenomenon could be undertaken, it might well prove possible to establish a typology of reactions.

Willingham, a Cambridgeshire parish on the edge of the Fens, seems to have produced a positive reaction which, superficially at least, bears a close resemblance to that posited for north Arden.[7] It is thought to have experienced a 25% population growth between 1575 and 1603 – from 100 to 125 households. In the second decade of the seventeenth century, however, there occurred what looks like a Malthusian check, with a falling off in the frequency of baptisms, and particularly high mortalities in 1613 and 1617. There were no less than 60 deaths in the latter year, which must have represented something like 1 in 10 of the population. But the growth regime was subsequently resumed so that by 1664 Willingham was successfully supporting 135 households.

As in Arden, the newcomers — 'men whose names do not appear in earlier surveys' — consisted mainly of landless cottagers, some with common rights, some without. By 1603, 54% of the local community was landless. As in Arden, too, the population growth was accompanied by radical agrarian changes: not only drainage and enclosure, but an expansion of barley production – barley was sown in the winter cornfield – and the development of dairying and cheese-making on a large scale. Meanwhile industrial employment became increasingly widespread. Fifteen out of 55 surviving wills dated 1575–1603 were those of craftsmen — weavers, carpenters, ropemakers and shoemakers.

Adapting a term used by Dr E. A. Wrigley,[8] this barley, cheese and craft-response might be regarded as one of the basic 'high pressure' solutions to ecological difficulties. The Shropshire parish of Myddle, recently studied by Dr D. G. Hey, provides an example of a 'low pressure' solution.[9] Here there was a traditional pastoral economy, not very dissimilar from that which obtained in north Arden prior to 1570. But it persisted for much longer in a state of undisturbed ecological equilibrium. Over the period 1561–1600, when the populations of Willingham and north Arden were growing fast, that of Myddle 'seems to have been only just maintaining its level, and this despite the arrival of a group of immigrant labourers in the 1580s and 1590s'. But then, during the 1630s, 'a second wave of immigrant labourers, much larger than the first, began to enter the parish'. By 1672 there were 91 households, an increase of 37 over the figure for 1563.

According to Dr Hey, however, this 70% population growth did not precipitate any significant agrarian changes. Local farmers continued to concentrate on the rearing of cattle, dairying and beef production as they had in the past. Some increase in industrial activity did occur. In the mid sixteenth century 1 in every 9 men had followed a craft; by the mid seventeenth century the proportion had risen to 1 in 7. But in absolute terms this would have meant only 7 additional craftsmen. And although Dr Hey speaks of the newcomers as 'labourers', it is difficult to see how a pastoral economy could have provided a great deal of regular work for the remaining 30 recently established householders. The main factor which enabled Myddle to support its extra numbers —and indeed, to support them relatively comfortably — was the presence of an ample supply of unappropriated land. Labourers seem invariably to have had smallholdings, plus common rights, which meant that to a considerable extent they were able to provide for their own subsistence.

A similar reaction is found in the south Arden parish of Rowington: except that here newcomers were accommodated not on waste land but by 'the fragmentation and division of holdings'. The manorial survey of 1548 suggests that there were then about 51 tenants, of whom 14 were small husbandmen farming between 5 and 19 acres, and 4 were cottagers. By 1649 there were 103 tenants in all, the new holdings having been created by 'the re-arrangement of existing farms', some of which had been divided and others 'clipped of small acreages'. Forty people now had 5–19 acre farms, while the number of cottagers with holdings of $4\frac{1}{2}$ acres or less had increased from 4 to 34.[10]

Myddle and Rowington represent variations of what might be regarded as the classical 'medieval' reaction to demographic pressure: the reaction which had been tried and found wanting in the fourteenth-century Malthusian crisis. Yet even in the seventeenth century, one imagines that wherever rural parishes were able to provide settlers with sizable landholdings there would have been a strong tendency for positive ecological adjustments to proceed no further. Only where a significant body of landless cottagers established themselves, perhaps, would a drastic change in the local economy — i.e., a 'high pressure' positive reaction — be called for.

One type of negative reaction — or at least, of reaction which was negative so far as the local community itself was concerned — seems to be exemplified by villages on the western clay plateau of Cambridgeshire. The population history of the clay villages', says Dr Spufford, 'was very different from those on the fen-edge, and many, though not all, of them shrank during the sixteenth and seventeenth centuries'.[11] At Orwell there was continuous natural increase between 1570 and 1650, but 'the community remained approximately the same size'. This parish, then, refused to support additional numbers. On the contrary, 'holders of traditional farms of a half-yardland or a yardland were squeezed out', while there was a corresponding increase in the size of larger holdings, and 'a tremendous expansion of the demesne, which may have absorbed the commons, as well as the arable of some of the tenants'. Some of the displaced husbandmen remained in Orwell as cottagers, but many born in the parish were left with no alternative but to emigrate, thereby transferring Orwell's ecological difficulties elsewhere.[12] However, taking a wider view, it might be argued that such a parish, while failing to support additional numbers itself, was responding to the national ecological predicament on an extra-parochial basis: for by rationalizing agricultural production, it was increasing the overall food supply and enabling extra mouths to be fed in its marketing areas. This type of negativity would therefore need to be distinguished from another kind — an example of which is not, however, at present known to me — in which a community, in reply to the ecological question, simply said 'no, full stop' — i.e., remained unchanged, not only in population size, but in economy and social structure.

III That the high degree of demographic mobility which is a marked characteristic of the late sixteenth and early seventeenth centuries was due in part to 'air flows' of landless people moving away from local communities which could not support them towards rural parishes and urban centres which could.

IV That this 'crisis' mobility may well have affected the timing of demographic crises in one locality as against another.

Although the evidence is slight, it is possible, for instance, that the movement of people in the late 1600s and early 1610s from the area affected by the Midland Revolt into North Arden parishes helped to precipitate the 1613—19 crisis (see p. 17).

Much of the movement must have been relatively local: from Feldon to Arden in Warwickshire, from clay plateau to fen in Cambridgeshire. But the apparent chronology of crisis (see *I*) rather suggests that, despite the obvious pull of London in the reverse direction, there may have been an overall tendency for some of the surplus population to flow from the South East Lowlands to the North West Highlands. However, other explanations of the chronology are possible — e.g., that because of the existence of more marginal land in the Highlands, this part of England was later in reaching saturation point than the always more densely settled South East. Surname study might well throw light on this issue.

V That among the factors which helped to determine a particular local community's reaction to ecological difficulties were the following:

(a) *The availability of waste land for the building of cottages, with or without smallholdings.*
Hence the long-recognized attraction of fen and forest areas at this time.
(b) *The seigneurial and tenurial situation.*
This factor was of particular significance at Chippenham where it was seigneurial policy to enlarge and consolidate tenures by the squeezing out of small copyholders;[13] and in a diametrically opposite way at Rowington where the fragmentation of traditional holdings was extensively practised.
  Closed villages prevented the settlement of squatters. Locally the tiny parish of Elmdon came into this category, its population remaining more or less static throughout late Tudor and Stuart times. Open parishes, on the other hand, which tended to be large — like Solihull and Yardley — permitted, or at any rate were unable to prevent, settlement.
(c) *The ability of a community to produce more cheap food than heretofore — usually as a result of agrarian change. And/or*
(d) *The presence or proximity of the resources necessary for the development of industrial employment.*
Parishes particularly well favoured from this point of view — e.g., on developing coalfields — often proved capable, not merely of absorbing their own population growth without crisis, but of attracting and supporting large numbers of immigrants. In Warwickshire itself, Bedworth, on the East Warwickshire coalfield provides a good example. In 1656 Dugdale speaks of it as being 'a place very well known in regard of the local mines there'. By 1730 Dr Thomas reported that 'in this Parish is a place call'd Colly Croft, lying half a mile full north from the Church, which by the resort of miners to the great coal works here, has grown into a regular compact village, consisting of above thirty houses'.[14] Such parishes became 'job providers' on a regional, or even an extra regional basis: complementing, as it were, other parishes which specialized as 'food providers' — i.e.,

parishes producing an exportable surplus of corn or arable produce – like Orwell or Chippenham.

VI That in certain circumstances, the price rise engendered what amounted to an injection of capital into a rural community; and that this surplus wealth could play a significant role in fostering agrarian change and industrial development.

It is interesting in this connection that Dr Spufford, when discussing Willingham, speaks of 'the impression left by the wills . . . of the prosperity and purchasing power wielded by those who held a conventional tenement'[15] – a remark which suggests that the surplus capital of the landed peasantry may have been as instrumental in stimulating positive responses there as was the case in north Arden.

VII That, since freeholders benefited particularly from the price rise, it would seem possible that, other factors permitting, parishes which contained a high proportion of freeholders were more likely to solve their ecological difficulties internally than those which did not.

VIII That a successful reaction to ecological difficulties may often have resulted in a polarized local community. But that this 'indirect' or 'contingent' polarization – i.e., contingent upon population growth – ought to be distinguished from 'direct' polarization, resulting from engrossment, eviction, etc.

The concomitance of polarization with population growth may turn out to be one of the most readily identifiable indicators of positive ecological reaction.

13

THE 'GENERAL EUROPEAN CRISIS'

It was as long ago as 1954 that E. J. Hobsbawm first advanced the concept of a general European crisis in the seventeenth century: a crisis which, 'in view of the wide variation of the periods of maximum disturbance in different parts of Europe', he has since suggested might well be taken as having persisted in some countries down to 1720.[1] While admitting that an explanation which would meet with general agreement still remains to be found', Professor Hobsbawm himself views this crisis as essentially economic, believing that it will eventually be seen 'to fit most readily into some elaborated or modified version of the Marxist model of economic development'.[2] In 1960 H. R. Trevor-Roper advanced a rival hypothesis, namely that the general seventeenth-century crisis was first and foremost of a political nature: 'a crisis not of the constitution nor of the system of production, but of the State, or rather, of the relation of the State to society'.[3] It was left to French historians to emphasize 'the number of bad harvests, of subsistence crises, of famines, of plagues';[4] and to infer from the widespread occurrence of such phenomena that both 'the long series of cumulative economic crises' and the 'series of political revolutions' may have been underlain by a much more fundamental, albeit elusive, malady: namely, an endemic Malthusian imbalance between population and resources.

This deeper insight derived from the intensive regional studies undertaken by French scholars, most notably by Le Roy Ladurie on Langedoc and Goubert on Beauvaisis. For his own contribution to the 'Crisis in Europe' debate, the latter contented himself — somewhat enigmatically, it must have seemed at the time — with '. . . A Regional Example'.[5] By the 1660s in the 38 parishes on which Goubert's study was based wage-earners nearly always constituted an overwhelming majority of the inhabitants. Typically, such people held a few acres of land on which they could grow 'enough to feed a family for a few months or a few weeks a year'. Otherwise, they had to do 'seasonal, and occasional jobs' for members of the landed peasantry; or alternatively, try to take up a craft occupation, as a cooper, wheelwright, tailor or weaver. In a dozen villages on the outskirts of Beauvais itself, many 'were engaged in carding and combing wool produced locally or imported from neighbouring districts', while elsewhere 'country weavers' operated under the putting-out system. Throughout the region there was an 'incessant search for other means of income', the cottager hunting 'for wool to spin, for lace to manufacture, for wood to chop, carve or sell, for any small job on the larger estates'.

Sufficient documentation is not available for Beauvaisis prior to the 1660s to permit Goubert to trace earlier developments with any degree of certainty. But from what little information is available he surmises that the population 'noticeably increased' between 1600 and 1647, 'despite a number of disasters of varying magnitude, such as a plague between 1620 and 1630 and a great food crisis in 1630–1.' By the middle of the century, however, the extreme limits of growth must have been reached. The five years from 1647 to 1651 brought a major demographic snarl-up, when 'the usual food crisis was . . . carried over (generally with increased intensity) from one year to the next'; with the result that there was 'a steep rise and heavy extension of poverty and mortality, and a sharp fall in births'. Briefer, but no less deadly, 'crises of subsistence' followed in 1661–2, 1693–4, and again in 1709–10. In a single year, between 10 and 15% of the inhabitants of a village would disappear, carried off by famine or epidemic. 'There can be little doubt', Goubert concludes, 'that these phenomena – and they are amply proven – express a kind of periodical disequilibrium between an irregular food supply and a prolific population, subject to fitful and uncontrolled increase.'[6]

As has already been pointed out, true crises of subsistence are thought to have been rare in this country. Nevertheless, the Arden evidence, in its milder way, certainly ties in well with the French view of the general European crisis; while at the same time implying that a remedial reaction may have been more easily achieved in England than on the other side of the channel.

Perhaps these findings also tie in well with a tendency which has been growing in British historiography of late – as exemplified, for instance, by Professor Beresford's reinterpretation of fifteenth-century depopulation and some of the recent writings on the early industrial revolution[7] – to see the traumas of economic and social change, not merely in terms of the struggle of class against class, man against man, but with a mindfulness of the wider, often sadder, yet surely essential, ecological perspective.

14

THE CIVIL WAR ALIGNMENT

An ecological account of the developments which culminated in the English Civil War would naturally concentrate on what Lawrence Stone has called 'the *pre-conditions*, the long-term social, economic and ideological trends that make revolutions possible'; rather than 'the *triggers*, the personal decisions and the accidental pattern of events which may or may not set off the revolutionary outbreak, and which are unique and unclassifiable'.[1] Professor Stone himself discusses the long-term trends that have most interested us under an apposite title: 'The development of disequilibrium, 1529–1629'. First and foremost, he calls attention to 'The doubling of the population in the 120 years before the civil war.' This 'is the critical variable of the period, an event the ramifications of which spread out into every aspect of the society and was causally related to major changes in agriculture, trade, industry, urbanization, education, social

mobility and overseas settlement'.[2] Second, as a result pre-eminently of
the price rise, but also of the dissolution of the monasteries and other
factors, there was 'a massive shift of relative wealth away from Church and
Crown, and away from both the very rich and the very poor towards the
upper middle and middle classes'.[3]

Keying these developments into the 'crisis . . . of the State' would require
a detailed knowledge of the way in which, and the extent to which, the
'long-term social, economic and ideological trends' affected the political
attitudes of a wide range of people occupying various positions in the
socio-economic hierarchy. This of course is baying at the moon; and certainly relevant documentation is so sparse and superficial for north Arden
that only the crudest appraisal is possible.

In terms of 'Ranks, Degrees, Titles', the gentry of the area covered a wide
spectrum. Easily the most prestigious seigneurial lords were the Digbys
who, in addition to holding Coleshill, Sheldon and Marston Culy, posses-
sed the vast estates of the Earls of Kildare in Ireland: a circumstance which
must have placed them amongst what Trevor-Roper has described as the
'great gentry . . . "able to dispend" with comfort £2,000 or £3,000 a year'.[4]
Sir George Devereux of Castle Bromwich and Lyndon and Sir Robert
Fisher of Packington, Church, Hill and Middle Bickenhill were both baronets, while Sir Simon Archer of Tamworth and Solihull had been knighted
by James I. Thomas Grevis, esquire, of Moseley and Yardley, on the other
hand, although his father, Sir Richard Grevis, knight, had held the royal
office of 'deputy lieutenant to his majesty in his principalitie of Wales',[5]
had refused to purchase a knighthood at the coronation of Charles I. The
two lesser manorial lords in the locality, John Maine of Elmdon and
Marston Culy and William Noel of Knowle, styled themselves 'armiger'.
So also, among the non-seigneurial gentry, did the Warings and the
Greswolds, both of whose pedigrees are to be found in the 1619 Visitation
of the County of Warwick. Families like the Dods of Yardley and the
Acocks of Sheldon, by contrast, belonged to an expanding category of
small landowner who, while not qualifying for gentility as the heralds
understood it, had nevertheless by the mid seventeenth century acquired
sufficient wealth and social standing to be popularly regarded as 'gentlemen'.

The extent to which the price rise affected the economic circumstances
of local lords depended largely on the tenurial situation on their estates.
In the smaller, predominantly copyhold manors like Sheldon and the
Bickenhills, it was relatively easy — given time — to adjust rents upwards
in the wake of inflation. The fact that copyhold rents varied from 1d. to
3s. 7½d. per acre at Knowle in 1605 shows that such adjustments were in
progress.[6] Alternatively copyhold land was sometimes converted to lease-

hold tenure. Only 3 out of 74 inventories dated 1530—69 specify unexpired leases, their total value amounting to £22 10s. By the 1610—49 period leases occur in 18 out of 80 inventories and account for £473 6s.[7] The majority of such tenures were for three lives or 99 years, but as time went on the 21 year term became increasingly common. In 1682 Sir Clement Fisher granted a 21 year lease on 80 acres in Church and Middle Bicken-hill at a rent of no less than £40 per annum. To a considerable extent at least, the Digbys, the Fishers, the Devereuxs, the Maines and the Noels were all able to safeguard the real value of their rent rolls by such man-oeuvrings.

On the large, predominantly freehold manors, however, the position was less favourable from the seigneurial point of view. Although nine customary farms at Solihull were turned into leaseholds between 1601 and 1632, the freehold land there, amounting to thousands of acres, re-mained frozen at a value of less than £15 per annum to the lord.[8] Likewise, in 1632 the Yardley rent of assize was estimated at a mere £25 17s.[9] Nor was there much opportunity for the lords of Solihull and Yardley to profit from agrarian change. Improvements were probably even more wide-spread on these manors than elsewhere; but the advantages accrued al-most entirely to the independent freeholders. Indeed, with their minuscule financial liabilities and total freedom to manage their holdings as they chose, the non-seigneurial gentry — together with the substantial yeomen freeholders who were pressing upwards to join them — undoubtedly bene-fited more from the demographic, economic and social changes of the sixteenth and early seventeenth century than any other socio-economic group.

But for a century and more, the freeman's gain had been the seigneur-ial lord's loss. So much so, that had the Archers and the Grevises been in possession of Solihull and Yardley thus long, they would have provided obvious examples of Trevor-Roper's 'declining "mere gentry"': land-owners who, unable or unwilling to 'improve' their estates, were so fin-ancially squeezed by rising taxation on the one hand, and the impact of inflation on the other, that they found it increasingly difficult to maintain their accustomed standard of living, and therefore — in the opinion of that commentator at least — provided a natural backbone to the rebel cause.[10] In fact, Solihull and Yardley were only acquired by their respective lords in the early 1630s, and the purchase price would presumably have taken into account the paltry returns.[11] Nevertheless, Thomas Grevis seems to have run into financial difficulties. He is known to have borrowed large sums of money, from a relative, Sarah Grevis of Guildford, and from John Whateley, a lesser gentleman of King's Norton, who forgave him a debt of over £300 in his will of 1638—9.[12]

Whether by chance or not, it is also a fact that the Grevises and the Archers were the only major seigneurial lords having a stake in the five parishes who did not identify themselves with the Royalists during the Civil War. Among other indications of opposition to the Crown, Thomas Grevis, having been fined £10 in 1632 for his refusal of a knighthood, was actively involved six years later in resisting Henrietta Maria's attempt to improve her royal manor of King's Norton by enclosing its extensive waste grounds; and in the war itself his younger brother, Richard, fought as a colonel for Parliament.[13] Sir Simon Archer, the antiquarian friend of William Dugdale, may not have been without sympathy for the king. Certainly, in 1644 he had to answer charges concerning his attitude to Parliament; and, after admitting to 'being enforced to send a man and a horse when Prince Rupert lay within a mile of his house', was duly removed from the Commission of the Peace, and not reinstated until 1650.[14] All the same, Dugdale's list recording the alignment of the Warwickshire gentry at the commencement of hostilities places Sir Simon among the neutral;[15] and in 1644 he himself pleaded that his estates had not been sequestered, that he had loaned money to the Parliamentarians, and that his eldest son, Andrew Archer, was serving as a colonel in the Roundhead army.

Overall though, with the Digbys, the Fishers and the Devereuxs espousing the Royalist cause, the big manorial families of the area broke 3 to 2 in favour of the king. The gentry beneath them were less loyal. John Maine of Elmdon and William Noel of Knowle adopted a neutral stance; and among the four non-seigneurial gentry whose position is known, so did Charles Waring of Berry Hall; while Robert Dod and William Acock both sided with Parliament. This left only Humphrey Greswold, with his ancient lineage and 467 acre, mainly copyhold rental at Greet, to join the baron and two baronets as 'A loyal subject of his Sovereign'.[16]

As far as can be ascertained, the Royalists had conventional religious views; and so probably did most of the local neutrals and Parliamentary supporters. The Grevises, however, were Presbyterians: starting with Sir Richard, particularized by Thomas Hall, the well-known Puritan encumbent of King's Norton, as 'a valiant and religious man' who sheltered 'conformable' Nonconformist ministers.[17] That Catholicism normally resulted in a Royalist alignment is highlighted by the fact that in the Gunpowder Plot country round Coughton, a few miles south of the five parishes, where the Papist recusancy rate in the Compton census of 1676 was between 20 and 25%, the gentry are recorded in Dugdale's list to have been Royalist to a man.

As an unshakable Catholic, this makes Charles Waring's neutrality all the more surprising. Siding with Parliament, one imagines, would have

been unthinkable for such a person. But why did he refrain from supporting the king? Among the likeliest deterrents, perhaps, was the excessive
weight of royal taxation. The collection of ship money was as deeply re-
sented in Warwickshire as anywhere else. In May 1636, nine months
after the serving of the writ, the sheriff reported that his petty constables
would not, or could not, force the inhabitants to make their assessments,
and he himself could not drag the information out of them. The rich were
shirking their responsibilities, with the result that an undue burden was
falling on the poor. By the end of the summer less than three-quarters of
the £4,596 demanded had been collected.[18] How much ship money Charles
Waring had to pay we do not know. But in the poll tax of 1660 his son
Thomas was charged £3. 8s. 0d. on an 'in terris' assessment of £170. This
meant that he had to find half as much tax as that due from the 63 other
Longdon taxpayers put together.

There are no means of establishing where the sympathies of the bulk of
yeomen, husbandmen and labourers lay: though the only two lowly par-
ticipants of whom we happen to have knowledge fought on the side of
Parliament. According to the Quarter Sessions records of 1657 John Prat
and Henry Price, both of Knowle, served as soldiers for the Common-
wealth and were 'maimed in that service'.[19] That there was strong grass-
roots support for the rebel cause in north Arden country is further suggested
by the fact that when in 1642 Lord Brook held meetings in each of the four
Warwickshire Hundreds for the view and training of volunteers on behalf
of Parliament, 'about 800 voluntiers, almost all well armed', appeared at
Coleshill, as against 'neer 800' at the staunchly Parliamentary Coventry,
650 at Warwick and 600 at Stratford.[20]

Some insight into the attitude of those 'rising' yeomen who favoured
Parliament may perhaps be gleaned from Walter Blith, the author of *The
English Improver*, published in 1650. The son of John Blith, a north Arden
yeoman who died at Allesley in 1626, Walter probably spent most of his
early life there and in the nearby parish of Coleshill; until about 1650, now
graced by the title of 'gent', he acquired an estate at Cotesbach, Leicestershire.[21] Blith was a totally committed Parliamentarian, serving as a cap-
tain in the Roundhead army and also as a sequestrator for Warwickshire
and a surveyor of Crown lands. In 1652 he dedicated 'The Third Impression much Augmented' of his book of husbandry, now entitled *The English
Improver Improved* to 'the Right Honourable The Lord General Cromwell',
and surmounted the title page with the legend 'Vive la Re Publick'. Nevertheless, there were limits to Blith's radicalism. Although he believed that
the poor 'ought to have advantages upon the Commons', he was not 'of
the Diggers minde'. Nor was he prepared to countenance 'the Levell Prin-
ciples of Parity or Equally which they seem to urge'; only 'this Parity . . . to

make the poor rich, and the rich richer, and all to live of the labour of their owne hands'.[22] To this end he stressed the paramount importance of creating full employment, holding up the Dutch as worthy of emulation in this respect. Indeed, one of the main arguments he advances in commending his 'Improvements' is that 'they will make work for the poore labourer'.[23]

Dr Joan Thirsk writes, 'the theme of his whole book of husbandry was that the plain farmer could, and should, take advantage of the ways now available to enrich himself by better, more productive farming methods'.[24] Thus Blith presses for as much enclosure 'as shall admit of no depopulation'; and strongly recommends the adoption of convertible husbandry, provided the land is not over-ploughed: 'Grazing fits for Ploughing and Corning, and Corning fits for Grazing; A most gallant opportunitie ... and prejudice whom, I would faine know: Abundance of poor set on work; Abundance of Corne raised.'[25] He also seeks 'to shew the way of Cow-keeping, Dayrying, or raising most Cheese and Butter';[26] and advocates hemp as 'a very good Commodity ... and Flax also', particularly as a means by which 'the poor in every Parish' may be maintained 'comfortably in a calling and livelihood'.[27] From Blith's point of view, the main menace on the rural scene was not the enclosing landlord or the tear-away yeoman, but 'your mouldy old leavened husbandmen, who themselves and their forefathers have been accustomed to such a course of husbandry as they will practise, and no other, their resolution is so fixed, no issues or events whatsoever shall change them'.[28] Holding these ideas on agriculture and rural society, and boasting as he does — with 'the Westerne parts of Warwickshire and the Northerne parts of Worcestershire' foremost in his mind — that 'the Wood-Lands' which 'were wont to be releeved by the Fieldon with Corne of all sorts ... now are grown as gallant Corne Countries as be in England',[29] one can readily recognize Walter Blith, the improver, as a product of his own locality; and it is possible that the broad lines of his political philosophy were also to some extent representative, at least of his own class of rising midland yeomen.

What, finally, can be said regarding the landless cottagers? It is conceivable that John Prat and Henry Price were of their number — we simply do not know.[30] In fact there is a total lack of local information about the political views of such people. Although during the dearth years of 1649 – 50 Digger colonies were formed in at least nine counties of southern and midland England, so far as the record goes, they approached no nearer to Arden than Wellingborough in Northamptonshire and Bosworth in Leicestershire.[31] Perhaps it is nevertheless a reasonable assumption that had Gerrard Winstanley's widely disseminated pamphlets reached the squatters of Yardley Wood or Shirley Heath, they could hardly have met with indifference. Richard Baxter, writing of the country round Dudley, 'where the woods and commons were planted with nailers, scythe-smiths and other iron-labourers', argued that 'there is usually found more knowledge and religion' among such people 'than among the poor enslaved husbandmen'.[32] And certainly, the famous Digger episode on St George's Hill, Walton-on-Thames — when a group of fanatics under Winstanley himself dug up the common and planted vegetables, only to be fined for trespassing and have their cottages pulled down — in its very abortiveness and futility, exactly expressed the predicament of our own John Rawlings and Humphrey Hodgetts. 'The whole Digger movement', writes K. V. Thomas, 'can be plausibly regarded as the culmination of a century of unauthorized encroachment upon the forests and wastes by squatters and local commoners, pushed on by land shortage and pressure of population.'[33] The problem of poverty in the seventeenth century, the Diggers were in effect saying on St George's Hill — and the Crown, in the form of the 4 acre act, for instance, had said the same long before — was the problem of landlessness. And so it was to remain until a completely new and different ecological phase had established itself, the phase which had its origin in the Industrial Revolution.

APPENDIXES

Appendix 1

THE PRACTICE OF BIRTH CONTROL

In his pioneer study of Colyton Dr Wrigley carried out a series of tests which were intended to confirm the practice of birth control within marriage. Several of these have been applied to the three reconstituted north Arden parishes, and although the samples obtainable were often too small to be regarded as anything more than indicative, it may nevertheless be useful to compare the results with the figures published by Dr Wrigley.[1]

1. At Colyton separate analyses of age-specific marital fertility for women marrying under and over 30 showed that in the 'family limitation' period 1647–1719 the latter had higher rates for all age groups (Table VIIa). Dr Wrigley inferred that this was because they had 'less reason to seek to restrict the number of their children' by the practice of birth control.[2] He did not, however, provide comparable figures for 1560–1646 or 1720–69.

In Arden communities the contrast in the fertility of older women according to whether they had married early or late is found during all periods (Table VIIb). If anything, it is slightly less marked for the 1600–24 generation, which is the one exhibiting the most emphatic concave marital fertility curve (p. 24).

There are of course several reasons why women marrying at 30+ would tend to be more fertile in their thirties than those who had married in early life. As Dr Wrigley himself points out, the interval between marriage and the birth of the first child can be expected to be short anyway.[3] By the same token, other early birth intervals will usually be shorter on average than those separating later children. Obviously women marrying at 30+ would be advantaged from the point of view of their childbearing rate by both these discrepancies, as against women who had married at −29.

2. Another pointer to family limitation adduced by Dr Wrigley concerns the age at which women in completed families bore their last child. At Colyton in the periods 1560–1646 and 1720–69, when the widespread practice of birth control is not suspected, this is much the same for women marrying at −29 as for those marrying at 30+, i.e., about 40 (Table VIIIa). But in the 1647–1719 period the mean age for women marrying at −29 was (1) significantly lower than for their contemporaries marrying at 30+, and (2) lower than for women marrying at −29 in both the preceding and following periods. Table VIIIb shows that (1) Arden women marrying at 30+ bore their last child on average considerably later than those marrying at −29 in all periods, and indeed, that this trait was less marked for the 1600–24 period than for 1575–99 or 1650–74; (2) that women marrying at −29 in the 1600–24 cohort bore their last child slightly later than their

111

TABLE VII   *Age-specific marital fertility related to age at marriage —Colyton compared with Sheldon. Solihull and Yardley (children born per 1,000 woman-years lived — figure in brackets gives number of woman-years on which the rate is based)*

(a) Colyton*

1647–1719	Age-group of wife			
	30–4	35–9	40–4	45–9
women marrying −29	265	146	96	0
	(215.5)	(191.5)	(146.0)	(108.5)
30+	316	284	116	43
	(38.0)	(67.0)	(103.5)	(92.0)

(b) Sheldon, Solihull and Yardley

1575–99	Age-group of wife			
	30–4	35–9	40–4	45–9
women marrying −29	285	207	135	29
	(101.5)	(72.5)	(44.5)	(35.0)
30+	571	222	233	78
	(10.5)	(63.0)	(30.0)	(25.5)
1600–24 women marrying				
−29	331	214	105	63
	(136.0)	(107.5)	(95.0)	(63.0)
30+	391	174	133	0
	(23.0)	(34.5)	(37.5)	(35.5)
1625–49 women marrying				
−29	365	216	163	36
	(167.0)	(134.5)	(116.5)	(83.5)
30+	432	343	125	33
	(37.0)	(67.0)	(56.0)	(61.5)

*See E. A. Wrigley, 'Family Limitation in Pre-Industrial England', *Economic History Review*, 2nd series, XIX, 1966, p. 92.

counterparts in the previous generation, though earlier than in the 1625–49 and 1650–74 generations.

3. Nor was the 1600–24 Arden cohort distinguished by the 'marked rise' in the interval between the penultimate and ultimate births which Dr Wrigley found at Colyton 1647–1719, and considered to be 'typical of a community beginning to practise family limitation'[4] (compare Tables IXa and IXb).

On the face of it one would expect an inhibition of fertility which was caused by food deficiency to affect this interval no less than family limitation. The reason the 1600–24 Arden statistic is unwarped is probably because last birth intervals can only be derived from completed families — i.e., those in which the wife attained the age of 45 in union or the union lasted 27+ years. Moreover for a

TABLE VIII   *Mean ages at the birth of the last child of women marrying under and over the age of 30 — Colyton compared with Sheldon, Solihull and Yardley*

(a) Colyton*

	−29	No of women	+30	No of women	Difference
1560−1646	39.8	50	40.5	25	0.7
1647−1719	37.6	22	42.7	14	5.1
1720−69	40.4	14	41.4	5	1.0

(b) Sheldon, Solihull and Yardley

	−29	No of women	+30	No of women	Difference
1575−99	35.2	12	42.8	6	7.6
1600−24	36.4	21	39.6	6	3.2
1625−49	37.4	22	40.0	10	2.6
1650−74	37.5	28	42.3	4	4.8

* See Wrigley, 'Family Limitation in Pre-Industrial England', 1966, p. 95.

family to be included in this analysis the wife either had to have married under 30 and borne 4 + children, or, if the age of marriage is unknown, to have had 6 + children, which is taken as implying marriage under 30. In an undernourished cohort few poor families would fulfil the above conditions, with the result that the 1600−24 statistic probably derives almost exclusively from the better-off, whose fertility one would not expect to be inhibited by malnutrition.

4. The bimodal distribution of final birth intervals demonstrated by Dr Wrigley for the 1647−1719 cohort at Colyton[5] is to some extent apparent in the 1600−24 north Arden cohort (Fig. 38). However, the second Arden peak (in the 48−53 and 54−9 intervals) comes earlier than in the Devon parish (54−9 and 60−5), while Colyton's long, thick tail, attributable largely to 'mistakes', is totally absent. The Arden distribution would therefore seem to be relatively natural.

TABLE IX   *Mean last birth intervals (in months) — Colyton compared with Sheldon, Solihull and Yardley*

(a) Colyton*			(b) Sheldon, Solihull and Yardley		
	Mean	No of last birth intervals		Mean	No of last birth intervals
1560−1646	37.5	76	1575−99	30.9	47
1647−1719	50.7	34	1600−24	27.7	56
1720−69	40.6	24	1625−49	27.8	48
			1650−74	30.1	67

* See Wrigley, 'Family Limitation in Pre-Industrial England', 1966, p. 93.

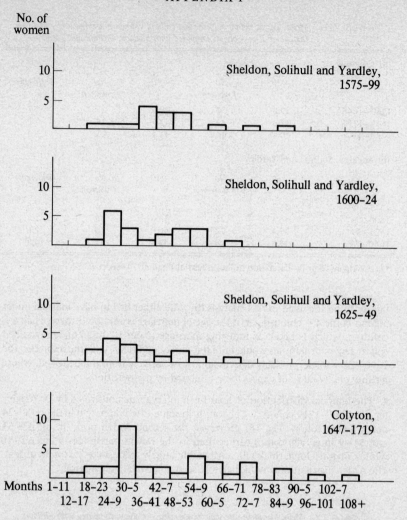

No. of women

Sheldon, Solihull and Yardley, 1575–99

Sheldon, Solihull and Yardley, 1600–24

Sheldon, Solihull and Yardley, 1625–49

Colyton, 1647–1719

Months 1-11 18-23 30-5 42-7 54-9 66-71 78-83 90-5 102-7
12-17 24-9 36-41 48-53 60-5 72-7 84-9 96-101 108+

Fig. 38. Number of months elapsing between the ultimate and penultimate births among women who married under 30 – Colyton compared with Sheldon, Solihull and Yardley

Appendix II

ESTIMATES OF POPULATION SIZE

The 1524/5 subsidy rolls for Bickenhill, Solihull and Yardley list a combined total of 247 taxpayers.[1] If a 60% allowance is made for omissions and exemptions (see Chapter 2, n. 7) this brings the total up to 395. It has recently been argued by Dr Patten that a figure arrived at in this way represents an estimate of males aged 16 + and that to convert this to an estimate of population size one needs to double it in respect of a presumed equal number of adult females and then allow for the fact that 40% of the total population are likely to have been children under 16.[2] A calculation using this method, however, provides a combined total of only 1,317 for Bickenhill, Solihull and Yardley in the 1520s. Quite apart from the problem of reconciling such a low figure with the earliest available Cox estimates, it would imply a population density of 1 person to 17.2 acres (or 1 household to 81.7 acres), which is patently unacceptable.

In any case, when one looks at the local rolls, Dr Patten's assumption that males who were over 16 but not householders are adequately represented, hardly seems tenable. Taking the returns for Solihull and Yardley together, out of a total of 169 surnames there turn out to be 149 which occur only once on their particular roll. Against this we find a combined total of 52 people bearing one of 20 duplicated names. Even in the extremely unlikely contingency of there having been no households in either parish which shared the same name, this would seem much too small a proportion of duplicates to account for anything like a full quota of sons over 16: for it would imply an average of less than one such person to every three surnames. Nor perhaps, on reflection, would one expect all males over 16 to be in receipt of a taxable income. Some of the sons of gentlemen and wealthy yeomen would doubtless have continued to receive support from their father beyond that age. Among the lesser peasantry many young men must have assisted their father on the family holding and/or in the pursuit of a craft: and as such are unlikely to have featured as wage-earners, least of all on a tax return. There is also the problem of sons who, while working as day labourers or craftsmen for a third party, would have continued to live at home. One would have expected the names of men of this sort to have been listed immediately after their father's; whereas in fact there is not one case of such a sequence on the Yardley roll and only five cases at Solihull. The many listed taxpayers who must have represented young men in the above categories, as well as their wives and children under 16, would be best treated not as individuals but as heads of households. Dr Patten's method in effect amounts to multiplying the number of taxpayers (plus an estimated number of omissions and exemptions) by 3.33. If, on the other hand, all taxpayers were taken as householders, a factor of 4.75 would be more appropriate (see below). Since it seems likely that the reality must have lain somewhere between these two extremes, an alternative procedure might be to use a factor half way between 3.33 and 4.75, i.e., 4.0. This

TABLE X   *Population estimates from taxation lists and religious surveys, with selected Cox estimates*

	Bickenhill	Elmdon	Sheldon	Solihull	Yardley	Total
1524/5 subsidy roll (taxpayers)	46			130	71	247
Population estimate	294			832	454	1580 (3 parishes)
1563 Bishop Sandys's return (householders)					135	
Population estimate					641	
1570s Cox estimate	230	60	227	1084	643	2244
1600s Cox estimate	312	75	375	1466	869	3097
1630s Cox estimate	306	75	359	1548	1150	3438
1663–74 hearth tax (householders)	100 (1663)	17 (1663)	61 (1674)	314* (1663)	211† (1667)	685
Population estimate	475	81	290	1492	1002	3340
1676 Compton census (communicants)	282	57	218	832	158	1547
Population estimate	470	95	363	1386	263	2577

*including Longdon 1662.
†allowing 22% for unlisted exempt households.

would give a population estimate for Bickenhill, Solihull and Yardley in 1525 of 1,580 as compared with a Cox estimate for the 1570s of 1.957. Without the adoption of some such formula it seems difficult to avoid the conclusion that 'the most comprehensive tax of the sixteenth century'[3] is locally so defective as to be useless for estimating population size.

The 1563 religious survey does not survive for the diocese of Lichfield, to which four of the five parishes belonged, but is available for Yardley which was with Worcester. Bishop Sandys's return for that parish records 135 households,[4] which if multiplied by the currently recommended factor of 4.75[5] gives an estimated total population of 641, as against a Cox estimate for the 1570s of 643.

The 1663–74 hearth tax returns[6] and the Compton census of 1676[7] are so close in date that cross checking is possible. When the total of householders given in the former is multiplied by 4.75 and the number of communicants in the latter increased to allow for children under 16,[8] we find that over the five parishes as a whole the Compton estimate falls short of that derived from the hearth tax by as much as 762, or 22.8%. Nevertheless this is mainly due to what is obviously an unacceptable Compton figure for Yardley, which yields a population estimate of only 263 as against the 1,002 implied by the hearth tax. Indeed, if we 'corrected' the Yardley figure to 1,002 in the Compton calculation, we should arrive at a five parish total of 3,317, as against the hearth tax estimate of 3,339 and a 1630s Cox estimate of 3,438. And although this correspondence masks a good deal of inconsistency between the Cox, hearth tax and Compton estimates at parochial level, it makes a figure of about 3,400 look at any rate the best guess for the combined population total of the five parishes in the mid seventeenth century.

For what it is worth, a comparison of the 1524/5 and 1663/74 estimates for Bickenhill, Solihull and Yardley suggests a population increase over six genera- tions of 1,389, or 88%. A similar comparison of the 1563 Yardley figure with the hearth tax estimate for the same parish implies an increase over four generations of 56%. The Cox increase for the five parishes between the 1570s and the 1630s is virtually the same, i.e., 53%.

NOTES

1. The National Background

1 Roger Mols, S. J., 'Population in Europe 1500–1700' in Carlo M. Cipolla, ed., *The Fontana Economic History of Europe, II: The Sixteenth and Seventeenth Centuries*, 1974, p. 38.

2 There are, of course, no means of knowing the exact periods and rates of population growth in the pre-industrial centuries (See Chapter 12, n.2); nor the precise population total at any given time. E. A. Wrigley suggests a population of just under 6 million for England and Wales over the period 1650–1700 (see Fig. 1, and E. A. Wrigley, *Population and History*, 1969, p. 78). On the other hand, D. V. Glass's revision of Gregory King's contemporary estimate puts the total at 5.2 million in 1695 (D. V. Glass and D. E. C. Eversley, *Population in History*, 1965, p. 204), which would imply a 1650 figure of just over 5 million.

3 J. D. Chambers, *Population, Economy and Society in Pre-Industrial England*, 1972, p. 5.

4 D. E. C. Eversley, 'Population History and Local History' in E. A. Wrigley, ed., *An Introduction to English Historical Demography*, 1966, p. 15.

5 Richard G. Wilkinson, *Poverty and Progress: An Ecological Model of Economic Development*, 1973, p. 58.

6 E. A. Wrigley, *Population and History*, 1969, p. 28.

7 The initial researches into the five north Arden parishes were carried out by a series of Birmingham University extramural classes under the author's direction, as follows: Sheldon, 1957–60 (see V. H. T. Skipp, *Discovering Sheldon*, 1960); Bickenhill, 1960–3 (see V. H. T. Skipp and R. P. Hastings, *Discovering Bickenhill*, 1963); Elmdon, 1960; Yardley, 1960–7 (see V. H. T. Skipp, *Medieval Yardley*, 1970); Solihull, 1960–7. The collation and further analysis of parochial data is being undertaken by the 'Land and Population in North Warwickshire' extramural class, which has been meeting at Solihull, under the author and Dr D. E. Gray, since 1967. The following students have made a substantial contribution to the work of this course: Miss A. J. Abery, Mrs P. M. Adams, Mr G. K. W. Arkieson, Mr H. Austin, Mrs R. Aveyard, Mrs D. J. Baylis, Mr J. P. Baylis, Mrs A. E. Bewick, Mr G. L. Bishop, Mrs K. Bowland, Mr D. Bryan, Mrs M. V. Buttery, Mr D. H. Cleasby, Mr T. England, Mr G. K. Foulger, Mrs G. Gibson, Mr E. W. Grimm, Mrs A. Harris, Miss A. D. Harris, Mr G. Harris, Mr R. N. Ingram, Mr M. E. Jones, Mr E. B. Lascelles, Mr S. C. Leonard, Mr R. A. McMillan, Miss J. M. Morgan, Mr E. Owen, Mr T. Parkes, Mrs S. A. Pedler,

Miss K. Proctor, Mrs J. Ratcliffe, Mrs S. Roberts, Mrs V. Samuels, Mr C. Scott, Mrs B. A. Shackley, Miss E. Sherwood, Mrs A. L. Skelding, Mr L. H. Skelding, Mrs C. Smethurst, Mrs K. J. Startin, Mrs M. C. Stephenson, Mr A. J. Stubbs, Mrs D. Tombs, Mrs R. Turner, Mrs E. M. Varley, Mrs K. Weller, Mr L. C. Wimpory, Mrs J. A. Woodall, Mr G. J. Wright.

2. The Local Setting

1 Survey of the Manor of Solihull, 1632, Bodleian Library, Ms. Top, Warwickshire, C3.
2 This figure is based on the subsidy roll for c. 1275 but allowance has been made for exemptions and evasions (see Skipp, *Medieval Yardley*, pp. 22—3).
3 R. S. Schofield, 'The Geographical Distribution of Wealth in England, 1334—1649', *Economic History Review*, 2nd series, XVIII, 1965, pp. 483—510.
4 Skipp, *Medieval Yardley*, p. 80.
5 *Ibid.*, pp. 81—2.
6 *Ibid.*, p. 98.
7 Based on the 1524/5 subsidy rolls for Bickenhill, Solihull (P.R.O. E 179/192/139), and Yardley (Birmingham Reference Library 392220, III, fo. 182). The estimate makes a 60% allowance for exemptions and evasions, a figure which is suggested by a detailed comparison of the Yardley roll with the first parish register (see Skipp, *Medieval Yardley*, p. 79 and p. 142, n. 3). It has recently been argued that taxpayers represent adult males over the age of 16, rather than householders — an issue which is discussed in Appendix II, p. 115.

3 The Ecological Approach

1 V. H. T. Skipp, 'Economic and Social Change in the Forest of Arden, 1530—1649' in Joan Thirsk, ed., *Land, Church and People: Essays Presented to Professor H. P. R. Finberg, Agricultural History Review*, XVIII, Supplement, 1970 (hereafter referred to as Skipp, 'Arden', 1970) pp. 84—111.
2 Survey of the Manor of Hampton in Arden, 1649, Birmingham Reference Library, 511984.
3 The best introduction to the ecological approach is Wilkinson, *Poverty and Progress*. The concept of ecological equilibrium is discussed pp. 21—2 and Chapter 3.

4 The Demographic Crisis of 1613—19

1 Family reconstitution for the parishes of Bickenhill, Sheldon and Solihull was carried out under the direction of Miss A. D. Harris, who also assumed responsibility for most of the statistical calculations. In general the procedures and conventions followed have been those used by Dr Wrigley (see E. A. Wrigley,

Family Limitation in Pre-Industrial England', *Economic History Review*, 2nd series, XIX, pp. 82—109, and E. A. Wrigley, 'Family Reconstitution' in Wrigley, ed., *Introduction to English Demography*, 1966, (Chapter 4). Where other conventions have been employed these are explained in the text or notes.

The parish registers of Elmdon and Solihull commence in 1538, that of Yardley in 1539, of Bickenhill and Sheldon in 1558. However, the Bickenhill register has no burials prior to 1582 and lacks a record of marriages between 1594 and 1681. The registers of Bickenhill, Sheldon and Solihull have year-long gaps or are seriously defective during the period 1649—53; and the same applies for Solihull and Yardley in all or some of the years from 1660 to 1664, at Elmdon and Yardley from 1666 to 1670 and at Bickenhill from 1672 to 1673. Aggregative analysis and family reconstitution have also revealed appreciable under-registration at Yardley between 1626 and 1645 and in the 1670s, and at Solihull between 1655 and 1674. On the other hand, the standard of registration is particularly high at Sheldon, Solihull and Yardley in the first quarter of the seventeenth century. At this time, too, the Solihull and Yardley registers often give details of status or occupation, while the former also records addresses and specifies the burials of paupers, strangers and beggars. The Elmdon register has an average of only 6—10 events per annum and was therefore unsuitable for reconstitution; and Bickenhill also had to be excluded because of the lack of marriages in the period 1594—1681.

2 One would have expected birth intervals 1—4 to move in accord with other fertility statistics, i.e., to be longer for the 1600—24 marriage cohort. Presumably the reason this is not the case is because the birth intervals analysis is by definition confined to completed families with 4 + children, if the female age of marriage was under 30, and 6 +, if it is unknown. The average therefore only refers to relatively fertile families and may not be typical of the cohort as a whole.

3 The Cox estimate, with an adjustment to allow for recusancy and defective registration (see below) is used in this study to establish approximate population totals between the 1570s and the 1630s, when the standard of registration was good. The Cox method is based on the assumption that, when reckoned over a period of 10 years, the birth-rate of a pre-industrial population averaged 33.3 per 1,000 persons: a figure which corresponds closely to Gregory King's estimate of 32 per 1,000 (i.e., 1 birth for every 28 members of a population). This idea of a constant pre-industrial birth-rate has been ridiculed as 'an assumption of heroic dimensions' (R. S. Schofield, 'Some Notes on Aggregative Analysis in a Single Parish', *Local Population Studies*, V, 1970, p. 14); and the Cox estimate is quite properly considered useless for general demographic purposes. Nevertheless, within the five parishes, family reconstitution suggests that fertility rates were fairly constant for the cohorts marrying in the periods 1575—99 and 1625—49 (see p. 13), and the much lower readings of the 1600—24 cohort were almost certainly due to the exceptionally unfavourable conditions of the 1610s (see pp. 23 ff.). During this decade the birth-rate was anything but average, and the Cox estimate would obviously be misleading. But otherwise — although the birth-rate may not have been 33 per 1,000 and it would therefore be wrong to place too much confidence in the actual figures

cited — it is felt that this ancient method may at least be taken as providing a rough indication of short-term fluctuations. In any case, the long-term trend can be confirmed from other sources. Figures for all available taxation lists and religious surveys have been tabulated in Appendix II (Table X, p. 116), together with the estimates of population totals which have been derived from them, and selected Cox estimates.

The Compton census of 1676, and work on recusancy carried out under the direction of Mrs J. Woodall, suggest that the proportion of Papists and Non-conformists at Solihull was as high as 12.5%, though in the other parishes the figure is likely to have been nearer 5%. It is also clear that recusants only very rarely presented their children for baptism. Thus 438 indexed sixteenth- and seventeenth-century Solihull Papists have only 8 'certain', 7 'probable' and 26 'possible' baptisms which may be linked to their names; and 58 Nonconformists 10 'possible' baptisms. It was therefore decided to make a 12.5% allowance for recusancy and defective registration at Solihull and a 5% allowance for each of the other 4 parishes. (N.B. In Skipp, 'Arden', 1970, a uniform 5% correction factor was used and this accounts for the discrepancies between the population totals given in that article and in the present work.)

4 The harvest year is taken to run from August to July and bears the date of the calendar year in which it begins. Live conceptions are reckoned at 9 months prior to the date of baptism. Elmdon was excluded from parts of the aggregative analysis because of its small size and the low number of events recorded in the register. Aggregative work on demographic crises has been undertaken by Miss A. J. Abery, Mrs K. Bowland and Mrs S. Roberts.

5 Evidence regarding the tenurial status of Solihull inhabitants is derived mainly from the Survey of the Manor of Knowle, 1605 (P.R.O., LR 2 228. 548), and the surveys of Solihull manor dated 1570, 1581, 1601, 1629 and 1632 (Bodleian Library, Ms. Top. Warwickshire C 3), all of which have been transcribed by Mr G. L. Bishop. Details of parish officers, pew rents and recipients of Wheatly's dole were obtained from the Solihull Church Book, also transcribed by Mr Bishop. Although this bears the cover inscription 'A Book containing the Accounts of the Parish Bailiffs and Sundry other Particulars beginning in the Year 1525 and ending in the Year 1657', certain entries in fact run on to 1720.

The value of inventoried estates (for the present purpose) was taken as the total value of all goods and chattels, and average values were worked out by twenty-year periods — see Chapter 9, n. 10; also Skipp, 'Arden', 1970, p. 86, n. 4, and p. 99, n. 3.

6 Wrigley, *Population and History*, p. 124.

7 Thomas McKeown, *The Modern Rise of Population*, 1976, pp. 23—4.

8 McKeown, *Modern Rise of Population*, p. 23.

9 C. J. Harrison, 'Grain Price Analysis and Harvest Qualities, 1465—1634', *Agricultural History Review*, XIX, 1971, pp. 135—55.

10 Early seventeenth century (undated) memorandum, Warwick Record Office, CR 299/14.

11 Peter Laslett, *The World We Have Lost*, 2nd edition, 1971, p. 118.

12 On the concept of 'ecological disequilibrium' and its ability to stimulate economic development, see Wilkinson, *Poverty and Progress*, Chapter 4.

5 Negative Responses

1 The corrected Cox estimate for the 1610s works out at 2,592, which would imply a cut-back of over 16%; but this is unacceptable for reasons given in Chapter 4, n. 3, p. 120.
2 Solihull Court Rolls, British Museum Additional Rolls 17771—82.

6 The Ecological Problem

1 Skipp, 'Arden', 1970, p. 86.
2 The Custom of the Manor of Knowle, 1635, Birmingham Reference Library, 379610.
3 Richard Carew of Antony, The Survey of Cornwall, ed. F. E. Halliday, 1953, p. 138.

7 Positive Responses: Agrarian Change

1 Skipp, 'Arden', 1970, pp. 86—99. The collection of 1530—1649 inventories which were used for this and other purposes consisted of 81 Yardley inventories, 10 Rowington (Diocesan Record Office, Worcester), 25 Bickenhill, 50 Sheldon, 51 Solihull (Joint Record Office, Lichfield). Statistics derived from inventories dated 1650—1725 were based on a further 73 inventories (25 Bickenhill, 5 Rowington, 5 Sheldon, 37 Solihull, 1 Yardley), supplemented for certain purposes — e.g., the price indices of cattle and arable crops — by further Rowington inventories and a substantial collection relating to Hampton-in-Arden. Inventory analysis has been carried out under the direction of Mr H. Austin and Mr A. J. Stubbs.
2 Skipp, 'Arden', 1970, Table V, p. 92.
3 Ibid., p. 93 and Table VII, p. 94.
4 William Camden, Britannia, ed. Edmund Gibson, 1695, p. 510.
5 Hampton survey, 1649.
6 Survey of the Manor of Forshaw, 1652, Warwick Record Office, CR 645/19.
7 Knowle survey, 1605; Skipp and Hastings, Discovering Bickenhill, p. 24.
8 Knowle survey, 1605; Solihull survey, 1632; Hampton survey, 1649.
9 For further details, see Skipp, 'Arden', 1970, p. 96.
10 Ibid., pp. 97—8.
11 The Agrarian History of England and Wales, IV, 1500—1640, ed. Joan Thirsk, 1967, pp. 857 and 861.
12 Michael Kingman, 'Markets and Marketing in Tudor Warwickshire: The Evidence of John Fisher of Warwick and the Crisis of 1586—7' (forthcoming).
13 John Pound, Poverty and Vagrancy in Tudor England, 1971, p. 50.
14 Carew, Survey of Cornwall, p. 102.
15 The proportion of inventories specifying winter corn, growing or garnered, declined from 59% in the period 1530—49 to 34% in the period 1600—49; meanwhile the proportion of inventories specifying oats and barley increased from 22% to 32%, and from 14% to 37% respectively.

16 Skipp, 'Arden', 1970, Table II, p. 88.
17 *Ibid.*, pp. 88, 91—2.

8 Positive Responses: New Employment Openings

1 Carew, *Survey of Cornwall*, p. 103.
2 Pound, *Poverty and Vagrancy*, p. 13.
3 Poll Tax of Knowle in T. W. Downing, *The Records of Knowle*, 1914, p. 379.
4 Solihull Church Book, pp. 191 ff.
5 Unfortunately, poll tax returns have not been traced for other local parishes.
6 Warwick Record Office, CR 299/678.
7 Joan Thirsk, 'Farming Techniques' in Thirsk, ed., *Agrarian History of England and Wales*, IV, Chapter 3, p. 177.
8 Knowle survey, 1605.
9 Skipp, *Medieval Yardley*, pp. 94—5.
10 R. A. Pelham, 'The Migration of the Iron Industry towards Birmingham during the Sixteenth Century', *Transactions and Proceedings of the Birmingham Archaeological Society*, LXVI (1945—6), p. 149.
11 A petition from West Midland metal workers against the engrossing of iron, 1603, see J. Thirsk and J. P. Cooper, eds., *Seventeenth Century Economic Documents*, 1972, pp. 188—90.
12 W. B. Bickley, Collections for Yardley, Birmingham Reference Library, 392220, IV, fo. 268.
13 E. F. Schumacher, 'Industrialization through "Intermediate Technology'" in Ronald Robinson, ed., *Developing the Third World: The Experience of the Nineteen Sixties*, pp. 85—93.
14 Ronald Robinson, ed., 'Technology, Employment and Culture: Cambridge Conference Report', in Robinson, ed., *Developing the Third World*, p. 102.

9 Model of Demographic Economic and Social Developments, 1575—1649

1 On 11 see p. 75.
2 Christopher Hill, *Reformation to Industrial Revolution*, Pelican edition, 1971, p. 87.
3 Alan Everitt, 'Farm Labourers' in Thirsk, ed., *Agrarian History of England and Wales*, IV, Chapter 7, p. 435.
4 *Warwick County Records*, II, 1936, p. 207.
5 Solihull survey, 1632.
6 For a further discussion of rents and also of entry fines, etc., see Skipp, 'Arden', 1970, pp. 106—7.
7 L. A. Clarkson, *The Pre-Industrial Economy in England, 1500—1750*, 1971, pp. 58—9.
8 Christopher Hill, *Reformation to Industrial Revolution*, p. 86.
9 *Ibid.*
10 Skipp, 'Arden', 1970, p. 103. Although this analysis was by forty-year periods, in order to take account of inflation, the average value of goods and chattels was worked out on a twenty-year basis. Wealthy peasants are those whose

inventoried goods and chattels were valued at above twice the average figure for the twenty-year period in which they died; substantial peasants between average and twice average; middling peasants between average and half average; lesser below half average.

11 In 1658 Robert Haywood, a Solihull carpenter, was paid 10s. 4d. 'for makeing ye Cucking-stoole, etc.' (Robert Pemberton, *Solihull and its Church*, 1905, p. 136).

12 Thirsk, ed., *Agrarian History of England and Wales*, IV, p. 608.

13 The Poor Law Act of 1601, A. E. Bland, P. A. Brown and R. H. Tawney, eds., *English Economic History: Select Documents*, 1914, p. 380.

14 *Ibid.*

15 Worcestershire Quarter Sessions, 1593—1643, calendared by J. Willis Bund, Birmingham Reference Library, 156300, 556/219.

16 *Warwick County Records*, IV, 1938, p. 73.

17 Yardley Parish Accounts, Memoranda and Lists of Parish Officers, Birmingham Reference Library, 278091.

18 Solihull Church Book, pp. 250 ff.

19 *Warwick County Records*, II, 1936, pp. 242—3.

20 *Ibid.*, IV, p. 95.

21 John Burman, *Solihull and Its School*, 1939, pp. 8—11.

10 The New Ecological Regime, 1625—74

1 British Museum, Additional Rolls, 17771—81.

2 *Warwick County Records*, II, pp. 14, 27, 82.

3 *Ibid.*, pp. 187, 221.

4 *Ibid.*, pp. 242, 207.

5 W. G. Hoskins, 'Harvest Fluctuations and English Economic History, 1480—1619', *Agricultural History Review*, XII, 1964, p. 46.

11 The Social Cost

1 Warwick Record Office, QS 11/7, QS 11/5. Much of the work on the hearth taxes and social structure was undertaken by Mrs M. Varley.

2 The former figure implies an average household size among the exempt of 3.5, the latter 3.9.

3 Margaret Spufford, *Contrasting Communities: English Villages in the Sixteenth and Seventeenth Centuries*, 1974, pp. 70 and 72.

4 *Ibid.*, p. 75.

5 Sir John Clapham, *A Concise Economic History of Britain, from the Earliest Times to 1750*, 1963, p. 209.

6 Gregory King, 'A Scheme of the Income and Expense of the several Families of England Calculated for the Year 1688', *Seventeenth Century Economic Documents*, pp. 780—1.

7 Solihull Church Book, pp. 244—321.

8 Burman, *Solihull and Its School*, pp. 17 ff; Skipp, *Medieval Yardley*, pp. 116—17.

9 Solihull Church Book, p. 123.

10 *Ibid.*, pp. 248 and 339.

11 Bickley, *Collections for Yardley*, v, fo. 355.

12 *Ibid.*, VI, fo. 443.

13 Margaret Spufford, 'The Schooling of the Peasantry in Cambridgeshire, 1575—1700' in Thirsk, ed., *Land, Church and People : Essays Presented to Professor H. P. R. Finberg, Agricultural History Review*, XVIII, Supplement, 1970, p. 113.

14 Solihull Church Book, p. 339.

15 Knowle survey, 1605.

16 Churchwardens and Overseers Accounts, 1690—1742, Solihull Parish Chest.

17 *Victoria County History of Worcestershire*, II, 1906, p. 66.

18 *Warwick County Records*, VII, 1953, p. 253 and 262.

19 Alan Everitt, 'Nonconformity in Country Parishes' in Thirsk, ed., *Land, Church and People: Essays Presented to Professor H. P. R. Finberg, Agricultural History Review*, XVIII, Supplement, 1970, pp. 178—99.

12 General Propositions

1 Chambers, *Population, Economy and Society*, pp. 25 and 28.

2 Though it probably represents a majority opinion — see, for instance, Wrigley, *Population and History*, 1969, p. 78 — not all historians would accept the pattern of national population growth which has been assumed throughout this work. T. H. Hollingsworth suggests that the rate of increase was greatest between 1475 and 1556, and that 'renewed growth between 1560 and 1587 may have been retarded by later marriages', etc. He also places the population of England in 1600 as low as 4 million. Nevertheless, even for Dr Hollingsworth it was about 1600 that 'the high point just before the Black Death' was 'regained' — or, in other words, that the critical Malthusian breakthrough occurred. See T. R. Hollingsworth, *Historical Demography*, 1969, pp. 385—8.

3 Joan Thirsk, 'Enclosing and Engrossing' in Thirsk, ed., *Agrarian History of England and Wales*, IV, Chapter 4, pp. 233 ff.

4 David Palliser, 'Dearth and Disease in Staffordshire, 1540—1670' in C. W. Chalklin and M. A. Havinden, eds., *Rural Change and Urban Growth, 1500—1800*, 1974, p. 64; Alan D. Dyer, *The City of Worcester in the Sixteenth Century*, 1973, p. 28.

5 Spufford, *Contrasting Communities*, pp. 100 and 152.

6 Andrew B. Appleby, 'Disease or Famine? Mortality in Cumberland and Westmorland, 1580—1640', *Economic History Review*, 2nd series, XXVI, 1973, pp. 403—31; M. Drake, 'An Elementary Exercise in Parish Register Demography', *ibid.*, 2nd series, XIV, 1961, pp. 435—6; Laslett, *The World We Have Lost*, pp. 120 ff.

7 Spufford, *Contrasting Communities*, pp. 121—64.

8 Wrigley, *Population and History*, p. 140.

9 David G. Hey, *An English Rural Community: Myddle under the Tudors and Stuarts*, 1974, pp. 41—184.

10 Joy Woodall, *From Hroca to Anne*, 1974, pp. 54—8.

11 Spufford, *Contrasting Communities*, p. 94.

12 *Ibid.*, pp. 94—119.

13 *Ibid.*, p. 75.

14 Sir William Dugdale, *The Antiquities of Warwickshire*, 2nd edition, ed. William Thomas, 1730, pp. 119 and 122.
15 Spufford, *Contrasting Communities*, p. 144.

13 The 'General European Crisis'

1 E. J. Hobsbawm, 'The Crisis of the Seventeenth Century' in Trevor Aston, ed., *Crisis in Europe, 1560—1660*, 1965, p. 55.
2 *Ibid.*, p. 58.
3 H. R. Trevor-Roper, 'The General Crisis of the Seventeenth Century' in Aston, ed., *Crisis in Europe*, p. 95.
4 Roland Mousnier, J. H. Elliott and H. R. Trevor-Roper, 'Trevor-Roper's "General Crisis": Symposium' in Aston, ed., *Crisis in Europe*, p. 103.
5 Pierre Goubert, 'The French Peasantry in the Seventeenth Century: A Regional Example', in Aston, ed., *Crisis in Europe*, pp. 141—65.
6 *Ibid.*, p. 159.
7 M. W. Beresford and J. G. Hurst, eds., *Deserted Medieval Villages*, 1971, pp. 15—17; R. M. Hartwell, ed., *The Causes of the Industrial Revolution in England*, 1967.

14 The Civil War Alignment

1 Lawrence Stone, *The Causes of the English Revolution, 1529—1642*, 1972, p. 37.
2 *Ibid.*, p. 67.
3 *Ibid.*, p. 75.
4 H. R. Trevor-Roper, 'The Gentry 1540—1640', *Economic History Review Supplement I*, 1953, p. 52.
5 The tomb of Sir Richard Grevis, King's Norton church, Birmingham.
6 See p. 68.
7 Skipp, 'Arden', 1970, p. 106.
8 See p. 68.
9 Bickley, *Collections for Yardley*, III, f. 196.
10 Trevor-Roper, 'The Gentry' pp. 26ff.
11 It may have been out of the profits of office that Sir Richard Grevis purchased the manors of both Solihull and Yardley about 1629. However, he quickly sold the former, which had already changed hands three times since 1604 (on the first occasion for £1,080) to Sir Simon Archer — see Robert Pemberton, *Solihull and Its Church*, 1905, pp. 14—15.
12 Alison Fairn, *A History of Moseley*, 1973, p. 21.
13 *Ibid.*, pp. 21—2.
14 *Warwick County Records*, II, 1936, p. XXVII.
15 Northants County Record Office, Finch Hatton Collection, F. H. 4284.
16 Skipp, 'Arden', 1970, p. 106; Humphrey Greswold's memorial in Yardley church.
17 Fairn, *History of Moseley*, p. 24.
18 *Victoria County History of Warwickshire*, II, p. 447.
19 *Warwick County Records*, IV, pp. 27 and 31.

20 *Ibid.*, II, p. XXXII.
21 I owe this biographical information to Dr Joan Thirsk, who has kindly allowed me to see an early draft of a paper she is currently preparing on Walter Blith.
22 Walter Blith, *The English Improver Improved*, 1652, The Epistle to the Industrious Reader (unpaginated).
23 *Ibid.*, The Epistle to the Cottager, Labourer, or meanest Cottager.
24 Dr Thirsk's unpublished paper on Walter Blith, see above n. 21.
25 Blith, *English Improver Improved*, p. 99.
26 *Ibid.*, Epistle to the Industrious Reader.
27 *Ibid.*, p. 249.
28 *Ibid.*, Epistle to the Husbandman, Farmer or Tenant.
29 *Ibid.*, p. 82.
30 An Edward Price was taxed on one hearth at Longdon in 1663, and since Price is an unusual surname in the five parishes it is possible that Henry belonged to the same family. The only Prat household listed in the hearth taxes is that of Thomas Prat of Shirley End, who was recorded as exempt over the period 1663–74.
31 Christopher Hill, *The World Turned Upside Down*, Penguin edition, 1975, p. 124.
32 Hill, *op. cit.*, p. 44.
33 K. V. Thomas, 'Another Digger Broadside', *Past and Present*, 42, p. 58.

Appendix I The Practice of Birth Control

1 Wrigley, 'Family Limitation in Pre-Industrial England', *Economic History Review*, 2nd series, XIX, 1966, pp. 82–109.
2 *Ibid.*, p. 91.
3 *Ibid.*
4 *Ibid.*, p. 94.
5 *Ibid.*, p. 93.

Appendix II Estimates of Population Size

1 Bickenhill, Solihull, P.R.O. E 179/192/139; Yardley, Birmingham Reference Library 392220, III, fo. 182.
2 John Patten, 'Population Distribution in Norfolk and Suffolk during the Sixteenth and Seventeenth Centuries', *Institute of British Geographers Transactions*, 65, 1975, pp. 50–3.
3 W. G. Hoskins, *Provincial England*, 1963, p. 185.
4 T. R. Nash, *Collections for a History of Worcestershire* (1781–99), II, p. 478.
5 Patten, 'Population Distribution', p. 46; Peter Laslett, 'Size and Structure of the Household in England over Three Centuries, Part I', *Population Studies*, 1969, pp. 201–2.
6 Bickenhill, Elmdon, Sheldon, Solihull, Warwick Record Office, QS II/7, QS II/5; Yardley, Bickley, *Collections for Yardley*, III, fo, 184.
7 William Salt Library, Stafford, SMS 33.
8 Patten, 'Population Distribution', p. 59.

INDEX

References to Tables and Figures are indicated by an italicized page number.